INTERNET ACTIVITIES FOR SOCIAL STUDIES

CHALLENGING

Editor:
Charlene Stout

Editorial Project Manager:
Elizabeth Morris, Ph.D.

Editor in Chief:
Sharon Coan, M.S. Ed.

Illustrator:
Howard Chaney

Art Director:
Elayne Roberts

Art Coordination Assistant:
Cheri Macoubrie Wilson

Cover Artist:
Tina DeLeon

Product Manager:
Phil Garcia

Imaging:
James Edward Grace

Publishers:
Rachelle Cracchiolo, M.S. Ed.
Mary Dupuy Smith, M.S. Ed.

Author:

Shirley A. Gartmann, Ph.D.

Teacher Created Materials, Inc.
6421 Industry Way
Westminster, CA 92683
ISBN-1-57690-405-9

©1998 Teacher Created Materials, Inc.   Made in U.S.A.

TABLE OF CONTENTS

Introduction 6

Integrating Technology 7
   Classroom Benefits 7
   Basic Equipment 8
   Changing Roles 9
   Fitting It All In 10
   Unacceptable Material 11
      Policy Considerations 11
   Acceptable Use Policy 12
   Safety Issues 13
   Internet Safety Rules for Students 14
   Plan for Instruction 15
      Planning Suggestions 15
   Maximize Online Experiences 16

Implementing Internet Projects 17
   Project-Based Learning 17
   Implementing Projects 18
      Before the Start of the Project 18
      During the Project 18
      After the Project 18
      Evaluating Students' Internet Projects 18
   Technology Lesson Plan 19

Electronic Communication 20
   Electronic Mail 20
   "Keypal" 21
      Weekly Student Evaluation 21
   "E-mail" 22
      Rules for Using E-mail 22
   Writing E-Mail 23
      Writing E-mail in Style 23
   Free E-mail Sources 24
   E-mail Mailing Lists 25
      Mailing List Cautions 25

Exploring the World Wide Web 26
   World Wide Web Browsers 26
      Hotlinks 26
      Internet Addresses (Uniform Resource locators—URLs) . . 26
      Troubleshooting Addresses 27
   Evaluating Home Pages 28
   Web Page Evaluation 29

TABLE OF CONTENTS (cont.)

Searching on the World Wide Web 30
   Web-Crawling Engines 30
      Search Engines vs. Subject Directories. 30
   Defining Your Search 31
      Preparing a Keyword Search 31
   Ranking Search Engines 32
   Refining Your Search 33
      Summary of Boolean Operators. 33
   Search Engine Strategies 34
   Lesson 1: Searching Skills 35
      Activity Sheet S-1: *Choosing Good Keywords* 37
      Activity Sheet S-2: *How Can I Get Better Results?* 38
   Lesson 2: Advanced Searching 39
      Activity Sheet AST-1: *Advanced Searching Techniques* 40
      Activity Sheet AST-2: *Using Boolean Operators* 41

Maps and Map-Making 43
   Lesson 3: Finding Your Way with Map and Compass. 44
      Activity Sheet Map 1: *Tools for Working with Maps* 47

The Ancient World 48
   Lesson 4: Introduction to Ancient Civilizations 49
      Activity Sheet AW-1: *Introduction to the Ancient World* 50
   Lesson 5: The Seven Wonders of the Ancient World 51
      Activity Sheet AW-2: *What Were the Seven Wonders?* 52
   Lesson 6: Finding Out About the Ancient World 53
      Activity Sheet AW-3: *Investigating the Ancient World*. 54
      Activity Sheet AW-4: *Learn About Ancient Architecture* 55

The Ancient River Civilizations 56
   Ancient Egypt 56
   Mesopotamia 57
   Lesson 7: Ancient River Civilizations. 58
      Activity Sheet E-1: *The Growth of River Civilizations* 59
   Lesson 8: The Culture of Ancient Egypt. 60
      Activity Sheet E-2: *The Gods of Ancient Egypt*. 61
   Lesson 9: Touring the Pyramids 62
      Activity Sheet E-3: *Locate the Pyramids* 63
      Activity Sheet E-4: *Using Egyptian Hieroglyphics* 64

TABLE OF CONTENTS *(cont.)*

The Ancient Roman Empire 66
  Lesson 10: Introduction to the Roman Empire 67
    Activity Sheet RE-1: *Everyday Life in Roman Times* 68
  Lesson 11: Roman Gods and Goddesses 69
    Activity Sheet RE-2: *Family Tree of Ancient Gods* 70
  Lesson 12: Roman Mosaics. 71
    Activity Sheet RE-3: *Create Your Own Roman Mosaic* 72
  Lesson 13: The Roman Form of Government 73
    Activity Sheet RE-4: *The Structure of the Roman Government* 74

Ancient Greece 76
  Lesson 14: Introduction to Ancient Greece 77
    Activity Sheet G-1: *Everyday Life in Ancient Greece* 78
    Activity Sheet G-2: *Women in Ancient Greece* 79
  Lesson 15: Games of the Ancient Olympics. 80
    Activity Sheet G-3: *The Original Olympic Games* 81
    Activity Sheet G-4: *The First Olympic Events* 82
  Lesson 16: Introduction to Greek Architecture 83
    Activity Sheet G-5: *Ancient Architecture* 84

Medieval Times 85
  Lesson 17: Introduction to Medieval Times 86
    Activity Sheet MT-1: *Everyday Life in Medieval Times*. 87
  Lesson 18: Medieval Heraldry. 88
    Activity Sheet MT-2: *Make your Own Heraldry Shield*. 90
  Lesson 19: Medieval Castles 91
    Activity Sheet MT-3 *Design a Castle* 93

The World of the Vikings 94
  Lesson 20: Introduction to the Vikings. 95
    Activity Sheet V-1: *Viking Travel Routes* 96
  Lesson 21: Everyday Life in Viking Times. 97
    Activity Sheet V-2: *Viking Everyday Life* 98
  Lesson 22: Viking Ornamentation 99
    Activity Sheet V-3: *Create Your Own Viking Jewelry*. 100
  Lesson 23: Viking Runes and Futharks 103
    Activity Sheet V-4: *Write Your Name in Runes and Futharks* 104
  Lesson 24: Did the Vikings Explore North America? 105
    Activity Sheet V-5: *Were the Vikings in North America?* 106

TABLE OF CONTENTS *(cont.)*

Mesoamerica 107
   Lesson 25: Introduction to Mesoamerica 108
      Activity Sheet MA-1: *Comparing the Three Civilizations* 109
      Activity Sheet MA-2: *The Nazca Line Drawings* 110
   Lesson 26: The Mystery of the Maya 111
      Activity Sheet MA-3: *The Mayan Calendar System* 112
      Activity Sheet MA-4: *Mayan Hieroglyphics* 113
   Lesson 27: Introduction to the Aztec Culture 114
      Activity Sheet MA-5: *The Aztec Social Class System* 115
      Activity Sheet MA-6: *Learn to Play Patolli* 117

Ancient China 118
   Lesson 28: History of Ancient China 119
   Lesson 29: Everyday Life in Ancient China 120
      Activity Sheet C-1: *Ancient Chinese Family Life/Modern Life* 121
      Activity Sheet C-2: *Ancient China's Contributions to the Modern World* 122
   Lesson 30: The Chinese Zodiac—Earth and Animal Signs 123
      Activity Sheet C-3: *Exploring the Chinese Zodiac* 124
   Lesson 31: Learn to Speak a Foreign Language 125
      Activity Sheet C-4: *Speak in Mandarin Chinese* 126

Appendices 127
   Appendix A: *Browser Skills* 127
   Appendix B: *Netscape Basics* 128
   Appendix C: *Microsoft Internet Explorer Basics* 130
      A Quick Tour of the Internet Explorer 132
   Appendix D: *Glossary of Terms* 134
   Appendix E: *Bibliography of Internet and World Wide Web Resources* 139
      Individual Search Engines and Subject Directories 139
      Bibliography of Technology Books 140
      Bibliography of Content Area 142
      Bibliography of Computer Software 144

INTRODUCTION

With the growing use of computers in today's society, the need for instruction in classroom technology becomes more important. With the use of effective instruction, the computer becomes a tool to assist students and teachers accomplish their studies quickly, neatly, and efficiently in a more stimulating manner that prepares students for a computer-oriented world.

The purpose of *Internet Activities For Social Studies* is to provide the classroom teacher with effective instruction regarding Internet and World Wide Web resources that are relevant to parts of the upper elementary and middle school social studies curriculum.

The early sections of *Internet Activities For Social Studies* focus on the benefits of teaching with the Internet, answer the most often asked questions, and suggest ways to organize and incorporate the technology into your classroom. It provides ways to block unacceptable material and to ensure the safety of your students while on the Internet. Wall charts, detailed lists, evaluations, forms, and visuals aid understanding.

The later sections of *Internet Activities For Social Studies* offer concrete ideas to integrate technology into your studies of the "Ancient Civilizations of the World." Eight units containing background information, guided lessons, and activities have been included so you, the teacher, can select those most appropriate for your particular curriculum or time requirements. It is designed so you can do one lesson or a group of lessons. The activities for each topic emphasize the acquisition of basic content knowledge and provide hands-on experiences designed to enhance or expand that knowledge.

Language Arts activities related to the ancient world have not been included in this book. They can be found in the *Language Arts, Reading and Writing—(Challenging)* edition of this series.

You will note that there are no answers for the Activity Sheets in this book. This is due to the problem-solving approach advocated by the author. In some cases, there will be no right or wrong answer. In other cases where a specific answer is expected, group members should be asked to come to an agreement as to which one they think is accurate. Students in the middle grades should be capable of validating their own knowledge.

In order to maximize teachers' and students' online time, a large number of addresses have not been included in the text. Instead, you will sometimes be asked to search for particular topic addresses. This will be a more flexible approach since web sites are known to "disappear" or be "down" at regular intervals. It should also ensure that the sites will be current since most search engines update their listings daily (or weekly, in some cases).

Be sure to check the Appendix section at the back of the book. To facilitate faster, more efficient use of the Internet, Appendices A, B, and C contain introductory sections on Browsers Skills and the basics of using the Netscape and Microsoft Internet Explorer. If your students do not have previous experience with the Internet, be sure to have them review and do the activities in these sections. Appendix D offers a glossary of computer terms. The most commonly used search engines and subject directories to help you find information quickly, accurately, and completely are listed in Appendix E.

CLASSROOM BENEFITS

By using the Internet in your classroom, you and your students will be able to:

- go directly to the best source

- explore other peoples' ideas

- facilitate collaborative learning

- use telementoring selectively

- exchange information throughout the world

- locate and retrieve timely information as needed for your classroom

- access multimedia sources which would otherwise not be available to you

- access real-world data and information contained in various databases

- publish your works immediately

- reach larger audiences

- add a variety of instructional strategies

- expand and enhance communication opportunities

- experience success in learning to do research

- find a vast amount of instructional materials for use in your classroom

- prepare for inevitable future changes in our world

- convert your classroom into an information resource center in which you collect and share data with each other.

BASIC EQUIPMENT

This book cannot possibly contain everything that is available on the Internet and World Wide Web, but it will give you some excellent resources to explore for use in your classroom. To begin, you will need the appropriate computer hardware and software. These are the basic requirements:

Computer Hardware

- PC with a 486 or better CPU, or a Macintosh with a 68040 or better processor

- 8 MB of RAM minimum

- Hard drive with at least 1 meg of available space

- Color monitor

- Printer (at least a 24 pin dot matrix)

- Modem with a speed of at least 14,400 bits per second transfer rate (A 28,800 is better if you expect to be loading a large amount of graphic images).

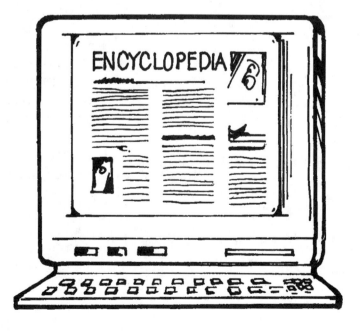

Computer Software

- E-mail software

- *Netscape* or *Microsoft Internet Explorer* Web Browser Software

- Large screen projection unit, or an RF converter so you can project your computer screen onto a large screen TV for whole-class viewing.

CHANGING ROLES

As technology is integrated into the classroom, you, the teacher, will need to change some aspects of your teaching. No longer will you be simply the dispenser of knowledge, but rather, you will become a facilitator and guide for student learning. In the same way, the curriculum will change to reflect students' interests as they make use of up-to-date information available through online sources. Teachers will no longer be limited to the resources in their classroom, school, or even their district. The entire world will be available to them as they exchange ideas and participate in collaborative projects with other teachers and with groups of students.

Just as teachers' roles will change, so will the ways that students acquire knowledge. Classrooms are already moving toward a "constructivist" approach in which students become involved in real world situations. Perhaps the most important skills to emerge from having the Internet in your classroom will be the thinking and problem-solving skills. Students must constantly make decisions in their data search. They must think critically and evaluate which resources offer the best information for their purposes. They must learn how to find and use appropriate information. Value judgements must be made to determine if the source of the information is valid and credible. Only then are they able to use that information to solve problems. In many instances, this can be done in a cooperative or collaborative learning environment.

For information on organizing, planning, scheduling, setting up, managing, assessing, and individualizing projects—all the things that make technology work in your classroom—see *Integrating Technology into the Classroom*. (Teacher Created Materials, Inc., Huntington Beach, CA.)

FITTING IT ALL IN

You will find the Internet useful to enhance your social studies curriculum relating to the ancient world through the lessons supplied for you in the last half of *Internet Activities For Social Studies*. Included you will find thirty specific lessons complete with teaching objectives, materials needed, Web sites, general information on the topics, specific steps for teaching the lessons, related activity sheets, suggested student projects, and extended activities, including other sites to explore.

Give yourself enough time to feel comfortable with the materials and the World Wide Web environment before you do a Web activity with your students or start an online project. In other words, make haste slowly!

The Internet is a good place for

- locating information not available in textbooks or the classroom/school library
- finding and contacting experts in a particular subject area
- utilizing government information which is not easily accessible outside of the Internet to the general public
- sharing information with other teachers and/or students from anywhere in the world
- publishing students' work online
- obtaining timely information (breaking news)
- reducing professional isolation by helping teachers keep in contact with professional colleagues worldwide
- helping students retain material
- gaining maximum educational value with limited time commitment.

The Internet is not a good place to

- find summaries or quick overviews of a topic
- replace hands-on activities such as drawing, writing, building, etc., although it can supplement these activities
- have active face-to-face interaction with other students and teachers.

UNACCEPTABLE MATERIAL

One of the biggest issues surrounding educational use of the Internet in schools is the question of acceptable use. There are many sites on the Internet which are unsuitable for viewing by children. The fear that students will access unacceptable material has limited the use of the Internet in some schools. To alleviate this problem, many school districts have developed an acceptable use policy which outlines the responsibilities of the individual user whenever he or she uses an Internet connection.

Policy Considerations

- Who will develop the responsible user policy— school personnel, administrators, parents, community members, students?

- What general district-wide and/or school-wide guidelines will determine who can use the online service, at what time, and under what circumstances?

- How can any restrictions be described and explained clearly and thoroughly?

- How can the policy be made as brief as possible— a clear, concise document with well-defined sections and topics?

ACCEPTABLE USE POLICY

In developing an Acceptable Use Policy:

- consider first adherence to any current local, state, or federal laws

- provide a description of the limitations of access, if any

- define authorized use and authorized access

- explain the responsibilities of anyone accessing the Internet through school facilities. This can include parent, students, teachers, support staff, groups meeting at the school, etc.

- define penalties for not abiding by the policies

- identify who can grant or revoke the privileges of net access

- provide information - particularly to students - about revealing personal information via the Internet or about meeting online acquaintances in person

- add signature lines for all users.

Once the policy is developed and ready to be implemented, be sure the information is shared with school personnel, community members, and anyone else who will be using the Internet. Copies should be distributed throughout the school and in appropriate information locations.

SAFETY ISSUES

Realize that the Internet is a neutral medium—culturally, racially, physically and with regard to gender. This can be an advantage to your students. However, the Internet has a dark side. It is also morally blind, making no judgements on what it passes on to the classroom screen. All you will know about the author of the data, or the other person you are communicating with, is what they reveal to you through the written message on the screen.

Just as we inform students about safety issues in dealing with strangers and potentially harmful situations outside the school, so too, we must let students know that there are some basic rules for online safety as well. The set of rules on page 14 was developed by the National Center for Missing and Exploited Children (1-800-THE-LOST) and the Interactive Services Association. They are included in a pamphlet entitled: "Child Safety on the Internet (1994)".

Since many of the activities available on the Internet can be done outside of school hours, parents will need to assume supervision of their children's use of the Internet. Many districts have a form that parents are required to sign indicating that they know the school's policy on general computer usage and Internet use specifically. A meeting with parents would also be appropriate—especially if you intend to do some kind of online project with your class. Getting parental cooperation is an important component for any successful Internet experience.

INTERNET SAFETY RULES FOR STUDENTS

1. **I will not give out personal information** such as my address, telephone number, parents' work number or address, or the name and location of my school without my parents' permission.

2. **I will tell my parents right away** if I come across any information that makes me feel uncomfortable.

3. **I will never agree to get together with someone I "meet" online** without first checking with my parents. If my parents agree to the meeting, I will be sure that it is in a public place and bring my mother or father along.

4. **I will never send a person my picture** or anything else without first checking with my parents.

5. **I will not respond to any negative messages** that are mean or in any way make me feel uncomfortable. It is not my fault if I get a message like that. If I do, I will tell my parents right away so they can contact the online service.

6. **I will talk with my parents so that we can set up rules for going online.** We will decide upon the time of day I can be online, the length of time I can be online, and the appropriate areas for me to visit. I will not access other areas or break the rules without their permission.

PLAN FOR INSTRUCTION

As with any instructional experience, successful use of the Internet and World Wide Web in the classroom involves advance planning. This planning is not that much different from the planning teachers ordinarily do for their regular classroom activities/lessons. Remember that planning is an ongoing process and you will need to plan for both long-range and short-term goals. The following list of suggestions can help you plan more effectively:

Planning Suggestions

1. Know why you are planning to use the Internet or World Wide Web. Have a written plan posted in your room.

2. Prepare your students in advance so they have a clear understanding of what you want them to accomplish as part of this experience. Explain your goals and objectives to them.

3. Check out the sites you want to access in advance so you have a reasonable assurance that these sites will be available at the times students will be looking for information.

4. Prepare for expected and unexpected outcomes. Have alternate sites ready which contain essentially the same information as your first choice of sites so you can send students to the alternate site if the first sites are unavailable.

5. Allow students enough freedom to pursue other links they may find during their "surfing." Monitor their activities to be sure they stay "on task" as much as possible, but allow them to follow some of their own choices. If they choose to go off on a tangent, have them make note of it and explain what they expected to gain from following that strand instead of the one that was assigned. (Sometimes the best learning occurs when it is unintentional.)

MAXIMIZE ONLINE EXPERIENCES

1. Ideally, the computer and phone line for Internet access should be within your classroom so you can monitor and assist students' activities while they are online.

2. Set up several activities to do within a specific time frame so students can move on to another activity if a server is down or the site is temporarily unavailable due to heavy traffic, weather, etc. (You should not be online during a thunder and lightning storm since it could damage your equipment. Usually the phone lines are not as reliable and your connection may be broken.) Another option is to download materials in advance using *Web Whacker* or *Web Marauder.*

3. Check to see if a site can be accessed through a gopher server (text only) or through the telnet command which may not be as heavily used.

4. Do a preliminary check on intended sites as close as possible to the intended time of day to determine if they are usually available at that time. Access is becoming more of a problem as students' use of the Internet increases.

5. Always give students some type of written response sheet to indicate how they spent their time online, or have them provide information about sites they visited.

6. Combine online with offline activities, particularly if you have limited access to an Internet connection.

7. Whenever possible, instruct students to turn off the automatic graphics loading option in their browser, or, if written materials are what you are most interested in viewing, have them select the text-based option if it is available at a site.

8. Providing you have a reasonably good, fast printer, consider printing out necessary information and viewing it offline.

9. Consider allowing students to do the assignment during another time of day, after or before school hours or at home if they have Internet access.

10. Remember that careful planning prior to doing an online project with students will greatly enhance your chances for a successful experience.

11. Plan enough exploratory time. These activities take more time than teacher-directed activities. Without enough time, students will feel frustrated and will find it difficult to stay on task.

12. Allow students to work in groups since this lets them share ideas, resources and tools.

13. Keep students focused and actively involved with the objectives of the activity by periodically asking them questions about the information they are finding:

    Is this information accurate and helpful in achieving the learning goal?

    Is all the information available at this site or do we need to look further?

    What should we do with the information we have found?

PROJECT-BASED LEARNING

One of the advantages of using the Internet in the classroom is that it gives you the ability to do project-based learning. In this situation, students can pursue some of their own interests while learning important skills which will be useful in their future professions. (One of the greatest hindrances to successful job performance reported by employers is the inability of some individuals to work in a cooperative/collaborative work environment.)

Project-based learning helps students develop problem-solving skills. They must make decisions in collaboration with the other students in their group about what information is needed and how it will be used within the project. The commonly identified elements of project-based learning are:

- in-depth inquiry
- collaboration
- contact with experts
- student-directed learning
- real-world problem-solving (interdisciplinary)
- real-life research
- publishing students' work and findings

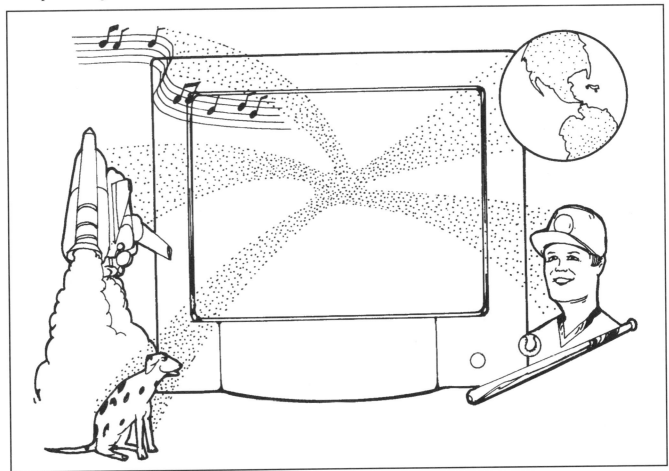

IMPLEMENTING PROJECTS

In setting up and implementing an internet-based project, careful planning is essential for the experience to be a successful one for your students. A brief listing of some important considerations for each part of the project are:

Before the Start of the Project

1. Design and test-run your proposed project.

2. Plan for realistic time frames.

3. Choose a time when teachers and students are not occupied with many other activities, such as the beginning and end of the semesters or holiday periods.

4. Remind participants of the beginning and ending dates of the project approximately one month before the project is scheduled to start. This should help you identify any individuals who may no longer be able to join your project.

5. Determine how you will compile the information. Develop any forms you may wish to use and pre-test them.

6. Plan enough time to answer a large amount of e-mail messages. Form letters will work best in some instances, so prepare them in advance. Whenever possible, involve students in the process.

During the Project

1. Share responses to your project with your students.

2. Have your students write short e-mail messages to each other to give them a better "feel" for what is involved in this type of project.

3. Check your e-mail regularly and post answers as soon as possible.

After the Project

1. Write a formal thank you to all project participants.

2. Have a formal plan in place to evaluate your project.

3. Share your results with project participants as well as other interested colleagues or write a magazine article, if appropriate.

Evaluating Students' Internet Projects

In most instructional activities, a student's learning must be evaluated and, where required, a grade must be given. Since many of these projects involve students working in groups, special problems arise in terms of determining each student's contribution to the success of the project. Most of these problems can be eliminated before the project is started if objectives and expected outcomes are carefully explained to the students.

TECHNOLOGY LESSON PLAN

Teacher/Class: _____

Subject/Specific Topic: _____

Teaching Objective: _____

Student Project: _____

Project Content: _____

Materials: _____

Web Sites: _____

_____

Preparation: _____

Teaching the Lesson: _____

_____

_____

_____

Extended Activities: _____

_____

Project Evaluation Plan: _____

_____

_____

ELECTRONIC MAIL

As our world becomes more technologically-oriented, e-mail and other forms of electronic information transfer will become an accepted way of communicating. E-mail is already gaining acceptance as a way of transferring information among schools and students. In the world of business, advertising and contact with associates via e-mail is commonplace. For students, even sending messages to their friends or relatives is instructional.

There are a number of curriculum-related activities that you can do with e-mail. For instance, you can get answers to questions about academic subjects, research topics for class reports, or just get another person's (or classroom's) perspective on a particular topic. In addition to learning about our own United States, you can explore and begin to appreciate differences in other societies, cultures, and countries. Personal connections made through e-mail can help you and your students broaden their viewpoints on any number of issues.

E-mail offers a number of potential activities which are relevant to the social studies curriculum. The first thing you as a teacher need to do is to locate "keypals" or "penpals" for your students. Some sources for such projects, as well as classrooms and individuals wishing to correspond with others, are:

Pen Pal Connection
http://alberti.crs4.it/pen-pal

E-Mail Key Pal Connection
http://www.comenius.com/keypal/index.html

Intercultural E-Mail Classroom Connection
http://www.stolaf.edu/network/iecc/

Your Mining Co. guide to Pen Pals for Kids
http://kidspenpals.miningco.com/msubpen.htm

Classroom Connect
http://www.classroom.net
This source also lists teachers seeking "keypals" for their students.

"KEYPAL"

Using e-mail in a "Keypal" activity is one of the least complicated activities you can use on the Internet. However, a successful student activity depends upon careful and thorough advance planning. Keypal's most common problem is too much unstructured time. To encourage students to stay on task, design a specific evaluation form (see below) to fit your needs.

A keypal activity is appropriate as an instructional strategy if you want to:

- connect students with an expert or mentor on a particular field

- practice a foreign language or learn about another culture or geographic location

- communicate information on relevant topics quickly

- learn how to write the researched information in a clear concise manner.

WEEKLY STUDENT EVALUATION

Project Title _____

Partners' Names _____

Starting Date/Time _____/_____ **Completion Date/Time** _____/_____

Keypal name _____ **Total Time Online** _____

Goals _____

Description of Activity _____

_____

_____

Questions That Arose _____

_____

_____

Problems Encountered _____

_____

Solutions to Problems _____

_____

"E-MAIL"

Prior to starting an e-mail activity, students should be made aware of some general rules and information about using e-mail properly and efficiently. One of the best sources for this is *The Net: User Guidelines and Netiquette* by Arlene H. Rinaldi. You can get a copy of this publication and other useful information on using e-mail at:

http://www.fau.edu/rinaldi/netiquette.html

RULES FOR USING E-MAIL

1. Never use all capital letters. This is equivalent to shouting.

2. Don't use inappropriate language.

3. Don't give out personal information (your phone number or address) even to someone you know since other individuals might have access to that information.

4. As a general rule, once you have read an e-mail message, save it to your local hard drive or floppy disk, then delete it to conserve on your e-mail service's hard drive space.

5. When replying to a message, it is often useful to include portions of the original message as a reference point.

WRITING E-MAIL

Writing good e-mail messages is somewhat different than writing letters. Because the messages are usually short or you are sending a reply to a previously-received message, there are style issues you need to think about.

WRITING E-MAIL IN STYLE

1. Write your message so that the receiver will be able to understand its meaning without having to guess.

2. Use meaningful subject lines so the receiver can quickly determine what the message is about.

3. Quote the e-mail message to which you are responding.

4. Use the person's name instead of pronouns.

5. Be aware of page layout issues:

   ➤ use short paragraphs

   ➤ keep the line length under seventy-five characters

   ➤ keep the messages under twenty-five lines

   ➤ use adequate white space

   ➤ use creative punctuation

   ➤ find replacements for gestures and intonation:

     • use smileys (found in the article in Appendix B)

     • put asterisks around sentences you wish to emphasize

     • use capital letters to emphasize

     • use lower-case letters when emphasis is not required

For additional information on this subject, read the article, "A Beginner's Guide to Effective E-mail" which can be found at: ducky@webfoot.com

---

FREE E-MAIL SOURCES

E-mail can be one of the easiest and most effective ways of introducing your students to the Internet and World Wide Web. To help individuals get on the Internet, *Juno Online Services* has made it possible to have free WWW e-mail accounts. In the author's opinion, this is the best free e-mail service, and it is the only one which doesn't require Web Access. Since Web-based e-mail systems have better graphics capabilities, they take longer to load. If you have been using your personal or school account to do e-mail activities with your class, having another e-mail account that is free would be advantageous.

Free e-mail Accounts

Juno	http://www.juno.com
Friendly E-mail	http://www.thekeyboard.com
GeoCities	http://www.geocities.com
GeoPlay	http://www.geoplay.com
Hotmail	http://www.hotmail.com
MailCity	http://www.mailcity.com
My Own E-mail	http://www.myownemail.com
NetAddress	http://www.netaddress.usa.net
RocketMail	http://www.rocketmail.com
Supernews	http://www.supercom

E-MAIL MAILING LISTS

One common way to get information from other people about a particular topic is to join a mailing list or listserv. Here individuals can post messages, and other readers can respond. If the list is unmoderated, anything goes. There is no "quality control." Moderated mailing lists have already been filtered before they are released to the general list subscribers.

Mailing List Cautions

1. A large number of messages are time-consuming to read. They may not provide any useful information.

2. Large amounts of hard drive space can be used up. This means that you will need a larger machine and faster processor.

3. It takes time to erase or print out these messages.

4. Mailing lists, like e-mail in general, are not private. This limits what you might want to say online or leaves your comments open to interpretation.

5. Mailing lists can sell your name and address to other mailing lists.

6. It is always harder to get off of mailing lists than to get on them.

WWW BROWSERS

Two of the most popular World Wide Web browsers currently used by schools are *Netscape Navigator* and *The Internet Explorer* because they were made available to schools free of charge or at a nominal cost. The author assumes that your students have some basic knowledge of the programs, but if memories need to be refreshed, this information has been included in Appendices A and B.

Hot Links is a WWW browser program used to navigate through various Internet sites. A hot link is a special area on the screen which is underlined or shown in a different color. The cursor changes to a crosshair or hand when over a screen hot link.

Internet Addresses (Uniform Resource Locators-URLs) have several parts which convey information necessary to get the message from one place to another. Let's take one apart:

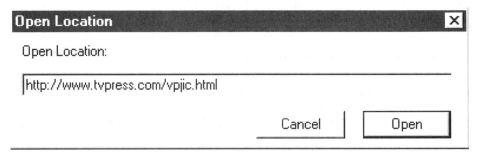

http://www.tvpress.com/vpjic.html

http:	at the beginning of the line identifies this as hyper text transfer protocol—which is the way information is transferred on the World Wide Web.
www.	indicates that this is a World Wide Web server. (You might also see a Gopher server or an FTP server.)
tvpress.	is the name of the host server which has the Internet software on it.
com	is the type of organization—commercial. Other organization codes: edu (education), gov (government), org (non-profit organization).
US	country designations for international hosts come after the organization code:

CA (Canada)	**AU** (Australia)
FR (France)	**UK** (United Kingdom)

vpjic	file name used to create the screen image
html	is the type of file—hyper text markup language

WWW BROWSERS *(cont.)*

The actual file used to create the screen image is found in the **HTML** *Hyper Text Markup Language* file. Anything that you see on an Internet screen must get directions from a file of some type. HTML is the most common language, although new languages for creating WWW pages are being developed. JAVA and CGI are new languages which are more powerful than HTML.

To access an Internet site, you will need the host address similar to the one shown above. To view a site online, type in the address exactly as shown with proper upper and lower case letters and all punctuation. *If you have difficulty accessing a site, just type in the first part up to the type of organization.*

http://www.tvpress.com/

This will usually get you to the home page for the site you are seeking. Then you will still have to look for the specific information you are seeking using instructions on the home page as your guide.

Troubleshooting Addresses

1. Check your spelling. Remember that all addresses must be entered exactly as written.

2. Shorten the address so you have only the essential parts for the first home page: http://www.anyserver.com/

3. Check to see if your keywords are appropriate for the information you are seeking.

4. Try some alternate sites. It is always a good idea to have more than one site for any activities you plan to use in the classroom.

5. World Wide Web sites are always changing. You may experience difficulty accessing a particular site. You might receive an error message like those shown below. Users new to the Internet and/or computers in general, often assume that they have done something wrong when they receive an error message. That is usually not the case. Unless you have mistyped the address, it is ordinarily a problem with the host server. Some error messages you might encounter are:

- file not found
- server down
- cannot find server
- the home page has moved to another server
- the server or home page is no longer operating
- the server is busy

6. In many instances, the server may not be up and running or may already have reached its quota of users. In this case, you should try again at a different time. Sometimes you can be successful in connecting if you try within the following five minutes.

EVALUATING HOME PAGES

As you become familiar with a number of World Wide Web pages, you will begin to identify certain features that make some *Home Pages* more appropriate than others for classroom use.

Following is a list of questions to help you identify which Web sites will be most useful.

1. **Is there intensive use of graphics?** This slows down the loading time. Limit graphics unless they are integral to that site information, as in an art site. Most sites begin with a graphic designed to attract the viewer's attention. This is followed by text information. European sites are primarily text with very little graphics.

2. **Is there a menu system? Can you follow the structure of the site easily? Are there options for returning to a home screen or other sections within the site?**

3. **Is the information at the site available in another, more traditional way?** If it is, there is little reason to spend your time online.

4. **Does the site show some degree of expertise?** Is it obvious that a teacher or other adult has been involved in developing and maintaining the site? Although many schools allow students to develop web pages, in many instances, they often lack the skills and knowledge necessary to do it strictly on their own, and the results may be less professional.

5. **Are there other marks of a good site?** (innovations, use of audio and/or video clips, use of interactive forms, links to external sites, etc.)

Once you feel comfortable using the WWW, help your students to evaluate Web pages so they will be able to make decisions about the information they are receiving.

WEB PAGE EVALUATION

Name of Web Page _____

URL Address _____

Yes/No   **COMMENTS**

_____ Appropriate use of graphics _____

_____ Text-only option _____

_____ Acceptable loading time _____

_____ Links to other sites _____

_____ Multimedia components _____

What topic/subject area might this page be most useful for? _____

Is this suitable for use with students?_____ teachers? _____ If no, why not?_____

_____

If yes, how do you think it could be used? (List subject that would be served by the site, age/grade level, and/or special needs.) _____

_____

List four positive things about this Web page:

1. _____
2. _____
3. _____
4. _____

How might the content on this Web page be improved?_____

_____

The best thing about this Web site is _____

_____

WEB-CRAWLING ENGINES

Imagine glistening spider webs spiraling from your computer with information web sites at each junction of the silken threads. See tiny train engines, propelling themselves on spidery legs, racing from site to site, searching out the most relevant information on your topic. This ridiculous but visual cartoon illustrates the concept of search engines.

Search Engines, Directories, and Hybrid Engines

Most search engines include a help section providing information about unique features and capabilities of that engine. Get acquainted with several search engines and directories in order to switch from one to another when access and response comes more slowly during the daytime hours. Study the chart below to see the advantages and disadvantages of each.

Search engines, sometimes called "crawlers" or "spiders," are constantly visiting and indexing Internet web sites, voraciously searching and often finding information that is not listed in directories. The most well-known, commercially-backed search engines, are usually well-maintained, dependable, and frequently updated to keep up with the ever-growing web. They include such names as **Alta Vista, ALL Net Find, Excite, HotBot, Infoseek, LookSmart, Lycos, Northern Light, Search.com, and WebCrawler.** See Appendix A for brief descriptions of each.

Subject directories are created by humans; therefore you may get better results from them. Instead of searching out information sites, directories categorize sites that are submitted to them. **Yahoo** is probably the best-known directory.

Hybrid search engines have an associated directory of sites that have been reviewed or rated available to users who ask to see the reviews.

SEARCH ENGINES	SUBJECT DIRECTORIES
* require more knowledge from the user * can be time-consuming * robot-driven index maintained by the computer * best for specific information * computer controls the searching pattern * can produce excessive results or "hits" if keywords are not well defined * keyword searchable * easy time saver for beginning web surfers	* sources preselected and index maintained by an expert in the field * focus is narrowed to relevant topics * keyword search allows more user control of the searching pattern * fixed vocabulary selected from established categories * sometimes contain keyword searches (not as capable as search engines)

DEFINING YOUR SEARCH

Effective use of keywords is one way that beginning surfers can define and narrow their search parameters. All search engines begin with some type of dialog box which allows you to type in a keyword or phrase.

With some engines, you can also select a boolean operator (see page 33) or customize your search by defining other parameters such as time periods or location.

The first step is to define the topic and the type of information you want to find as specifically as possible. Once you have identified the topic/content, you can choose appropriate keywords for your search. A diagram of this process is shown below.

Preparing for a Keyword Search

Define the Topic: _____

Identify Search Objective: _____

Choose a Search Engine or Directory: _____

Define type of information as general or specific: _____

Define Keywords:

keyword one	keyword two	keyword three	keyword four
_____	_____	_____	_____
_____	_____	_____	_____
_____	_____	_____	_____
_____	_____	_____	_____

Before you begin an online search, list the keywords you intend to use. Include possible synonyms for your topic. Since thinking of synonyms is sometimes difficult while you are online, it is important to do this ahead of time. Many newer search engines, such as Infoseek, list related topic areas to help you in the search process. However, this does not help if you are searching for a very specific item within a particular topic area.

RANKING SEARCH ENGINES

After trying several search engines, you can begin to make some judgments on which engine will work best for you. Knowing the features of each engine will help you make a better choice. The first consideration is the number of web pages and/or databases that are searched by the engine. **Hotbot** and **AltaVista** have the largest information bases, so you are likely to find more results using these engines. **HotBot** is the fastest engine; results are returned very quickly.

The real "acid test" for a search engine is not how many results they find but how many relevant sites they find. How a search engine "hits" (finds the matches) will often determine the relevancy of a particular result. This is influenced by where the engine looks for your keywords. An engine can search for keywords in a title, URL, the first 25 lines, or in the body of a document. Depending upon the database, you might miss a good site if the search engine does not look deep enough.

Different Methods of Ranking Results Used by Different Engines

Once the results are obtained, many engines use a ranking system to indicate how close the engine thinks a result is to the keyword(s) you have used. In this case, you will need to know how results are ranked. A ranking for a site is usually indicated by a percentage. Not all rankings are determined in the same way. **Yahoo**, a subject directory, determines their rankings in this way:

1. The highest ranking goes to the sites which match the most keywords.

2. Documents which have the keywords in the title are ranked higher than those which have the keywords in the body of the document or in the URL address.

3. The higher up the match in the category tree used by **Yahoo**, the higher the ranking.

Another popular search tool is **Infoseek**. This is really a hybrid search engine and subject directory since it has components of both. Their ranking percentage is called a "confidence level" with the most relevant matches appearing at the top of the list. Scoring is influenced by:

1. how near the beginning of a document the keywords are found (includes title)

2. the frequency of the keywords in the document

3. whether the keywords are "uncommon" and thus receive more weight in database.

The **Hotbot** search engine also uses a ranking system which is similar to those given above. The best possible match would be given a score of 99%. The other criteria are:

1. the frequency of keywords in the document

2. the finding of keywords in the title (that match receives a higher ranking)

3. If the keyword is found many times in a shorter document, it is ranked higher than if it is found many times in a longer document.

Knowing how different search tools gather and report information can help you determine which engine is best for you. You will still need to spend time experimenting with different tools to determine which one(s) gives you the most relevant results for your needs.

REFINING YOUR SEARCH

After you have done a keyword search, you may find that the information is not exactly what you wanted. This usually happens because you have not used keywords which are specific. Most search engines include a section on searching tips which can help you do more efficient searches. One frequently-used way of narrowing your search is to use *boolean operators*. These are similar to those used in mathematical logical expressions. Since all search engines do not use operators in the same way, or they may include the NOT operator, be sure to check how the operators are used in any online search engine you use. It is important to know how each one affects the results since they will not always be the same.

In many of the newer search engines, the actual boolean operators are not used. Instead, you may be given choices which have the same effect and meaning. For instance, a choice which indicates that a search will be done on "all the words" is equivalent to the AND operator. If, on the other hand, you select "any of the words", you will get many more results since this is equivalent to using the OR operator. The most limiting choice would be to use a PHRASE option which will only search for a sequence of words. Since the phrase option greatly limits your results, you will sometimes get an empty list.

Summary of Boolean Operators

Operator	Equivalent	Best Used For
And	all the words	narrowing the results within a specific topic/content area
Or	any of the words	browsing for large amounts of information
Phrase	all the words in the exact sequence of the phrase	specific results within a well-defined topic/content area
Not	(no equivalent)	eliminating possible double meanings for keywords

SEARCH ENGINE STRATEGIES

The effective use of appropriate search strategies and engines will greatly improve your results and reduce your time online. Some general tips to consider are:

1. Understand the difference between search engines and subject directories. Know when to use each one.

2. Try different search engines and be sure to read the "tips or help" sections.

3. When using a search engine, plan your search ahead of time and be as specific as possible.

4. If the search engine has a rating system (usually expressed as a percentage), select those results with a 90% or above rating since they are more likely to contain the information you are seeking. (If you have the time, you might want to look at the other addresses and descriptions as well since a good address might appear further down the list.)

5. Use double quotes (" ") to indicate a phrase so the search will look for that "group" of words.

6. If a word must appear in the results, put a plus (+) in front of it.

7. If you don't want a word to appear in the results, put a (-) in front of it.

8. Learn to use "wildcards" which allow you to search for strings of words or for differences of spelling within words. (Wom*n will find woman, women).

9. Use boolean operators to broaden or limit your search.

In the next section, you will find several activities which you can use with your students to develop and reinforce their understanding of World Wide Web searching tools and strategies.

LESSON 1

SEARCHING SKILLS

Help your students develop and improve their World Wide Web searching skills while finding information on the Vikings.

Materials: Web Browser (*Netscape, Microsoft Internet Explorer*, etc.)
Activity Sheet S-1: *Choosing Good Keywords*
Activity Sheet S-2: *How Can I Get Better Results?*

Web Sites:

Search Engines	**Directories**
http://hotbot.com	http://yahoo.com
http://altavista.digital.com	http://www.lycos.com
http://infoseek.com	

Meta Search Engines

http://dogpile.com   http://Allinone   http://savvysearch

Preparation: Students should be familiar with general concepts related to using WWW search engines and directories for finding information (See previous section). If this lesson is done as a group activity, students should be familiar with instructional group set up and operation in a classroom setting.

Teaching the Lesson:

1. To determine students' prior knowledge of the Vikings and their culture, use the concept map (Activity Sheet S-1: *Choosing Good Keywords*) to list keywords for possible searches. This can be done as a group activity or it can be done individually. As a result, a compilation of keywords can be made and presented in class.

2. Review the basic ideas related to using keywords for finding information on the WWW (defining keywords, use of synonyms, narrowing the search, etc.).

3. Divide the students into groups of four or less. Follow these steps:

    * Identify preassigned group members.

    * Have students use Activity Sheet S-2: *How Can I Get Better Results?* to record their results.

    * Explain that students will need to find words or combinations of words which are directly related to the Viking history and Nordic culture. Some examples are:

Viking Ships	Viking Explorers	Viking everyday life
Scandinavia	Viking Museum	Sweden
Viking Jewelry	Viking Gods	Norway
Viking Clothing	Viking Money	Denmark
Vikings in America	Viking Weapons	Vikings in England

LESSON 1

SEARCHING SKILLS *(cont.)*

Use as many examples as necessary depending upon the available time and students' experience.

4. Suggested questions to stimulate students' thinking:
   - Where did the Vikings live?
   - How did they get from place to place?
   - How did they live?
   - What were their beliefs?
   - Did they travel into other countries?

5. Have students work individually or in groups for about 10 minutes. They should record their keywords on Activity Sheet S-1: *Choosing Good Keywords.*

6. Reassemble the class and have students look at the keywords each group or individual has chosen. Reproduce the chart on the overhead or just write the keywords on the board.

7. Discuss why some choices are better than others (too narrow, too broad, repetitive, etc.)

8. After a short discussion, students should be sent to the computers to actually do the search. Even though some of the keywords they have chosen may not be the best choices, tell them to use the ones they have identified. Knowing which keywords give unsuitable results is also important. They should use Activity S-2: *How Can I Get Better Results?* to record their results. As before, this can be done in groups or by an individual. Depending upon your World Wide Web access, this might be done as an out-of-class assignment, on a rotation system during class time, or during students' free periods.

Students can use this process to search for information on other topics after they have had several experiences with search engines and begin to feel comfortable with using them.

Students can be assigned specific topics for which to search for information or students can be allowed to search for information on subjects of their choice. They can get practice using keywords by choosing another topic, defining the keywords and then going online and doing the search. For any search, they should document the search using Activity Sheets S-1: *Choosing Good Keywords* and S-2: *How Can I Get Better Results?* New topics and keywords should be entered on the sheets whenever a student does a new search.

Activity Sheet S-1:

CHOOSING GOOD KEYWORDS

Name _____

Directions In each circle below, fill in at least two keywords related to the topic—*Vikings*.
Choose the best keywords that you think will give you the most information.

keywords

keywords

Vikings

TOPIC

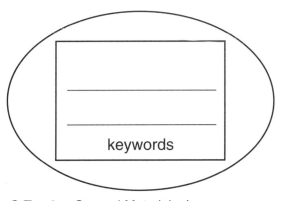

keywords

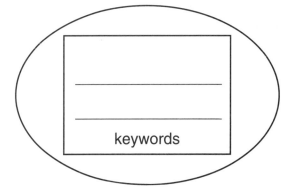

keywords

Activity Sheet S-2:

HOW CAN I GET BETTER RESULTS?

Name _____

After finding and studying the Web sites; answer the following questions:

1. Did using the topic word—"Vikings"—give you the results you expected? If not, explain why not.

   _____

   _____

   _____

2. What could you do to get better results?

   _____

   _____

   _____

3. When you look at the results, do you see any of the addresses repeated? If so, list them below. List the Search Engines you used:

   _____   _____   _____

   _____   _____   _____

   _____   _____   _____

   _____   _____   _____

4. Based upon your results, which engine do you think will be the best one for your search? Give your reasons why.

   _____

   _____

   _____

   _____

LESSON 2

ADVANCED SEARCHING

Help your students learn how to use advanced searching techniques to narrow their search results.

Materials: Activity Sheet AST-1: *Advanced Searching Techniques*

Preparation: Students should have experience doing simple searches using two or more search engines or subject directories. They should be familiar with using keywords for searches and with using the phrase option for searches.

Teaching the Lesson:

1. Choose a search engine that the students have used for past searches. Be sure to check for the availability of advanced search capabilities. Use the information on refining your search and boolean operators found in the beginning of this section to determine which advanced features are most useful for your students. (This may vary according to the topics and/or content area.)

2. Give students directions for Activity Sheet AST-1: *Advanced Searching Techniques*. Have students go online and complete the sheet.

3. When the first activity is finished, discuss some ways students found to narrow their searches, paying special attention to the differences between and among engines. Although some students may have used boolean operators, review the ways in which they can limit their search parameters by using the boolean operators—AND, OR or NOT—or equivalent phrases.

4. Direct students to complete Activity Sheet AST-2: *Using Boolean Operators* using a search engine of their choice.

Extended Activities:

Have students define and identify ways in which they might refine the following sets of keywords or use advanced search strategies to get more focused results:

castles	Egypt	Greece	civilization
culture	customs	United States	World History

Activity Sheet AST-1:

ADVANCED SEARCHING TECHNIQUES

Name _____

Name of search engine or subject directory _____

Keyword (s) or phrase used _____

Advanced Searching Technique used _____

Explain how this technique helps to give results:_____

_____

_____

_____

_____

Why did you choose this technique? _____

_____

_____

_____

Were the results what you expected? If not, is there a way to make your results more relevant?_____

_____

_____

_____

Activity Sheet AST-2:

USING BOOLEAN OPERATORS

Name _____

1. Enter a keyword in the appropriate place in your search engine. Do the search.

   How many matches (hits) were found? _____

2. Choose a second keyword that is compatible with the first keyword and enter the two words in the search dialog box. Record your results below:

   number of hits _____

3. Locate the "OR" operator, use the same keywords, and record your results below:

   number of matches _____

4. Using the circles A, B, & C shown below as a reference, answer these questions:

   Which of the search methods (numbers 1–3) gives you

   the least results _____why?_____

   the most results _____why? _____

5. Which operator would include the matches from circles A & B below?

6. What phrase would you use to get a listing of matches from circles B & C?

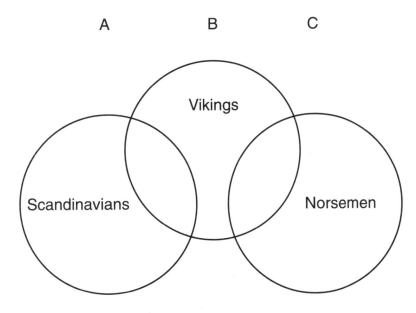

Activity Sheet AST-2:

USING BOOLEAN OPERATORS *(cont.)*

Name _____

1. Color in the appropriate circles if you used the keywords—Scandinavians and Vikings with the operator **AND**.

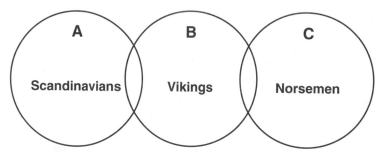

2. Color in the circles for the keywords—Scandinavians and Norsemen using the operator **OR**.

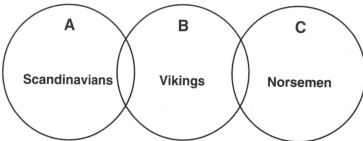

3. Color in the circles for the keywords Vikings and Norsmen using the operator **AND**.

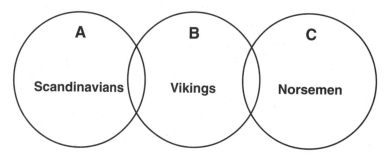

4. What would you color in if you used the phrase Scandinavian Vikings? _____

LEARN ABOUT MAPS AND MAP MAKING

Working with maps extends from the earliest civilizations to the present day. The United States Geological Service has produced a wonderful set of instructional materials on using maps and map-making for students in grades K-12. Some examples from these materials have been included in this book. The principles that underlie the use of maps can be incorporated into various social studies topics including history, geography, anthropology, and archaeology.

The Egyptians, Greeks, and Romans made maps from clay and papyrus. In general, Greek astronomers are credited with inventing latitude and longitude and identifying the location of the Equator. Even though we do not have examples of true maps from before 600 B.C., a great deal of experimentation and knowledge about maps and map-making preceded their actual development. The earliest precursor of a map that has been documented was found in the Ukraine and dates back to approximately 6200 B.C. It is a pictorial representation which has elements that can be identified as related to map-making.

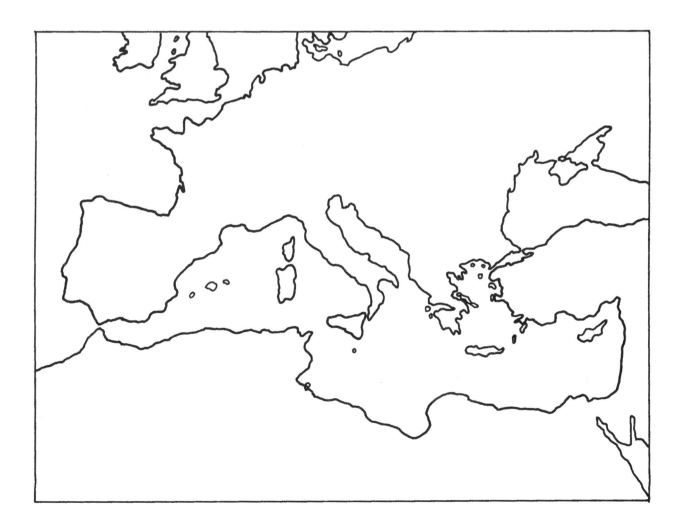

LESSON 3

FINDING YOUR WAY WITH MAP AND COMPASS

Introduce your students to terminology and concepts involved in using maps and a compass to find particular locations.

Materials: compass
Activity Sheet MAP-1: *Tools for Working with Maps*

Web Sites: http://www.usgs.gov/fact-sheets/finding-your-way/finding-your-way.html
http://www.nucleus.com/~dreamwvr/lost_civ.htm

Preparation: Since these lessons are adaptations of some lessons presented by the United States Geological Service, they have been condensed so they can be finished over a shorter time-period. If you wish to do more lessons or need additional material for a particular lesson, visit the site and print out the other lessons. Ask students to pay special attention to any vocabulary terms they encounter since they will likely be used in other lessons. They will also need to answer the questions on another sheet of paper. This will serve as a record for the teacher and student.

Topographic Maps

A topographic map tells you where things are and how to get to them, whether you are hiking, biking, hunting, fishing, or just interested in the world around you. These maps describe the shape of the land. They define and locate natural and man-made features like woodlands, waterways, important buildings, and bridges. They show the distance between any two places as well as the direction from one point to another.

Teaching the Lesson:

1. Have students log on to the "finding your way" site above.

2. Ask students what does "actual distance in the same unit of measurement" mean?

3. Have students study the web sites and with a partner make suggestions of what they can do in regards to map-making and navigating with a compass.

4. With their compasses, do the following activities for determining distance and direction.

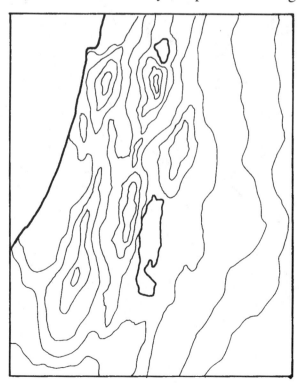

LESSON 3

FINDING YOUR WAY WITH MAP AND COMPASS *(cont.)*

Measuring Distances

Distance is measured between points on the map by aligning the scale with "0" on one point and extending the scale bar toward the other point. If these points are close enough to each other, you can read the number of feet or miles between them on the scale. If they are too far apart for that, put a strip of plain paper down on your map, and mark the strip where it touches the two points. Then match this marked strip with the appropriate scale printed in the margin of the map and figure the distance from a series of comparisons with the scale. Read the distance on a curving road or fence line the same way. Mark a strip of plain paper at the ends of relatively straight stretches of road or fence, and then compare the marked strip with the scale.

Determining Direction

To determine the direction, or bearing, from one point to another, you need a compass as well as a map. Most compasses are marked with the four cardinal points—north, east, south, and west—but some are marked additionally with the number of degrees in a circle (360°: north is 0° or 360°; east is 90°, south is 180°, and west is 270°.) Both kinds are easy to use with a little practice.

1. Take a compass bearing from a map:
   - Draw a straight line on the map passing through your location and your destination and extending across any one of the map borders.
   - Center the compass where your drawn line intersects the map border. Align the compass axis N-S or E-W with the border line and read on the compass circle the true bearing of your drawn line. Be careful to get the bearing in the correct sense because a straight line will have two values 180° apart. Remember north is 0°, east is 90°, etc.
   - To use this bearing, you must compensate for magnetic declination. If the MN (Magnetic North) arrow on the map magnetic declination diagram is to the right of the true north line, subtract the MN value. If the arrow is to the left of the line, add the value.

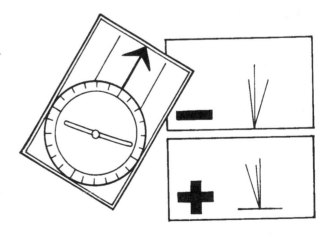

LESSON 3

FINDING YOUR WAY WITH MAP AND COMPASS *(cont.)*

A Word of Caution:

Compass readings are affected by the presence of iron and steel objects. Be sure to look out for, and stay away from, pocket knives, belt buckles, railroad tracks, electrical lines, and so forth when using a compass in the field.

Extended Activity #1:

If you wish, you can also have students create their own maps by going to one of the sites shown below:

Mapquest:	http://www.mapquest.com/
Map Creation Software:	http://lorenz.mur.csu.edu.au/cgi-bin/gis/Map
Online Map Creation:	http://www.aquarius.geomar.de/omc/omc_intro.html

Extended Activity #2

1. Using the information gained from the chosen site, have students make a map of their school and its grounds (determine an appropriate ratio—use paper).

2. In preparation for making their maps, using information gathered from the students' reading of the map-making materials, have students make a list of the decisions they will need to make regarding:

   • type of map

   • ratio (scale)

   • size of map

   • area covered by map

Activity Sheet MAP 1:

TOOLS FOR WORKING WITH MAPS

Name _____

Web Sites: http://www.usgs.gov/education/learnweb/Maps.html
http://www.nucleus.com/~dreamwvr/lost_civ.htm

Throughout history, tools for making maps have long been an object of human interest. Ancient mariners were forced to devise some kind of system for locating particular places and times or they could risk being lost forever. The early explorers in North America had to develop maps of the areas discovered so others could follow. The current emphasis on space exploration has made it necessary to map the Third Dimension. Time is another component that needs to be taken into consideration when plotting courses.

1. Log on to the USGS site and select "Location" on the first screen and then "Activity One: Tools of the Ancients" on the second screen. Read the onscreen information and do any activities as directed.

2. When you have finished with the Tools Activity, go back and select the "A Place in Time" option and do the activities as directed.

3. There are other map related activities under the other choices of "Navigation" and "Exploration" which might be of interest to you. If time and resources permit, you may wish to do these as well.

4. Use your favorite Search Engine/Directory to look for other references to mechanical inventions which were originally used to navigate, or work with maps and map-making.

5. List below any questions, problems encountered, and solutions to the problems.

_____

_____

_____

_____

_____

_____

THE ANCIENT WORLD

A recent Life Magazine article listed 100 major events which have changed the world during the last millenium. It included several events relating directly to the ancient world:

1. The establishment of a consistent calendar system was instituted by Julius Caesar in 46 B.C. and subsequently modified by Pope Gregory XIII in 1582. Eventually, the Gregorian calendar became the active calendar. However, it is not 100% accurate; it runs 26 seconds fast each year, leaving a margin of error of 6 days every 10,000 years.

2. The Olympic Games had originally been a tribute to the gods and a show of humanity's capability for grace, speed and strength. But they were discontinued in 393 A.D., having been corrupted by betting, bribery, cheating and professional athletes posing as contestants. When the modern Olympics were founded in 1896 A.D., attempts were made to reestablish the original purpose of the games. To a degree, this has happened, but commercialism and power struggles remain. The games however, do allow countries to focus their attention on the good in competing and winning.

3. The establishment of the modern university as a center of learning drew its inspiration from the teachings of Ancient Greece and Rome. A law school which adapted Roman Law to the contemporary needs of European society was established and still underlies our judicial system in this country and in Europe.

4. The seeds of democracy were planted in England by King John in 1215 A.D. when he signed the Magna Carta. It gave rights to citizens and promised due process to those accused of a crime. The initial ideas can be traced back to Ancient Greece.

5. The Crusades (1100-1300) began as a Christian Campaign to reclaim Jerusalem from Muslim rule. It ended up inspiring the creation of a wealth of art and literature which eventually led to the Renaissance.

6. The compass was discovered in China in the 4th Century B.C., but it did not make its way to Europe until around 1190 A.D. With the addition of the compass as a tool for navigation, sailors were able to sail the Mediterranean even when the skies were overcast and sun dials could not be used. This opened up a larger territory for exploration and promoted greater trade possibilities.

7. The splendor of Tenochtitlan was built in 1325 A.D. in Central American on a location which is today inhabited by Mexico City. It was unrivaled as an example of a planned city while Europe was still relatively unsophisticated.

8. Egyptian hieroglyphics were an enigma for many generations. Archaeologist were unable to translate their meaning until, in 1799, soldiers in Napoleon's army found a slab of basalt stone containing three languages including Egyptian hieroglyphics. The other two languages were Greek and Demotic (a simplified Egyptian script). If these two languages could be used to decipher the Egyptian Hieroglyphics, all of Egyptian Literature would be available for study. What scholars found was more than they could have dreamed. The Egyptians had extensive knowledge of medicine, astronomy, and geometry. They also had a sophisticated, well—organized form of government and an advanced weights and measurements system.

(Information given above taken from *Life Magazine*: "The Millenium." October, 1997.)

48

LESSON 4

INTRODUCTION TO ANCIENT CIVILIZATIONS

Give your students an overview of ancient civilizations, their location, everyday life and culture.

Materials: Activity Sheet AW-1: *Introduction to the Ancient World*

Web Sites: http://galaxy.cau.edu/tsmith/oldciv.html#globlang
http://ancienthistory.tqn.com/mbody.htm

Teaching the Lesson:

1. Introduce students to general information about the ancient world. (This can be found at http://galaxy.cau.edu/tsmith/oldciv.html#globlang, or one of the other sites if that one is not available.)

2. Do a demonstration of the site with the entire class, or have the students fill in Activity Sheet AW-1: *Introduction to the Ancient World* individually or in small groups of two to four students.

Extended Activities:

Some civilizations are considered "lost" because very little information about them has been recovered. One of these is the Atlantean/Minoan Civilization. To explore information about this civilization and related controversies concerning other "Lost Civilizations," visit the following site:

http://www.nucleus.com/~dreamwvr/lost_civ.htm

Students can also get information on The Perseus Project, which includes an excellent introduction to Greek and Roman Mythology and Classical and Mediterranean Archaeology.

The philosophy of the individuals running this site is best explained by the dedication that introduces it:

*Dedicated to those who explore mankind's past civilizations in
order to better understand the future of mankind.*

Activity Sheet AW-1:

INTRODUCTION TO THE ANCIENT WORLD

Name _____

Identify and give the location of five civilizations that were prominent in the Ancient World:

1. _____

2. _____

3. _____

4. _____

5. _____

On the timeline shown below, mark and label the approximate duration of the civilization's prominence. **(Note:** We will only be charting through Medieval times). The time span will be from 3000 B.C. to approximately A.D. 1100.

/ _____ /

starting date   present date
3000 B.C.

Other Sites to Explore:

Sumerian Mythology
http://pubpages.unh.edu/~cbsiren/sumer-faq.html

LESSON 5

THE SEVEN WONDERS OF THE ANCIENT WORLD

Help your students to identify the Seven Wonders of the Ancient World. Discuss their locations and their importance in the development of civilization.

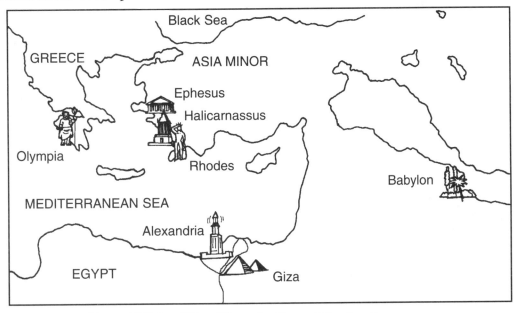

Materials: Activity Sheet AW-2 : *What Were the Seven Wonders?*

Web Sites: http://pharos.bu.edu/Egypt/Wonders/list.html

Teaching the Lesson:

1. Many of the achievements of ancient civilizations are known only through writings and pictures. Of the original Seven Wonders of the World, only one, the Great Sphinx, is still in existence. Ask students why they think these other wonders are no longer in existence.

2. Ask students why the ancient civilizations felt the need to make these large-scale monuments.

3. Ask students if they think civilization still has a need to create large-scale monuments. If so, have students give some examples of such monuments.

Extended Activities:

1. Ask students if there are any regions of the world where religion still promotes the building of large temples and other buildings. If so, have then give some examples.

2. Ask students what keywords they might use if they wanted to get additional information. Have them list several possible keywords related to the Seven Wonders of the Ancient World. Then have them do a search.

Activity Sheet AW-2 :

WHAT WERE THE SEVEN WONDERS?

Name _____

Using the information gathered from the Web site:
http://pharos.bu.edu/Egypt/Wonders/list.html
identify the Seven Wonders of the Ancient World and explain why they are "wonderful."

1. _____
   _____

2. _____
   _____

3. _____
   _____

4. _____
   _____

5. _____
   _____

6. _____
   _____

7. _____
   _____

List at least three modern-day achievements which might qualify as "wonders" of the modern world including explanations as to why you think they are worthy of being called "wonders."

_____

_____

_____

LESSON 6

FINDING OUT ABOUT THE ANCIENT WORLD

Provide your students with a simple introduction to archaeology and cultures of the ancient world.

Materials: Activity Sheet AW-3: *Investigating the Ancient World*

Activity Sheet AW-4: *Learn About Ancient Architecture*

Web Sites: http:/www.usd.edu/anth/midarch/arch.htm

Teaching the Lesson:

1. Archaeology is the scientific study of the cultures of peoples of the past. The purpose of archaeology is to understand how humans in the past interacted with their environment, and to preserve this history for present and future learning.

2. After reading the information from the "What is Archaeology?" site, students can do some exploration of their own into the world of archaeological investigation.

3. Archaeologists are really "detectives" of sorts. They must use their subject knowledge, coupled with scientific methodology, to determine as many pieces of information as they can about a particular excavation site or an individual artifact.

4. Most museums have an educational section which provides instruction and activities for teachers and students. The London (United Kingdom) Natural History Museum has two online activities—"The Cosmic Football and The Beast of Bodmin Moor"—which can be used to test your students' powers of observation and reasoning. Log on to the sites and see if they can solve the mysteries presented there. The address for the site is: http://www.nhm.ac.uk/index.html Remember that it is important for students to keep track of the information they have gathered.

Extended Activities:

Have students search these Web sites for additional information on the ancient world:

1. Rune's Ancient Coin Page: http://www.telepost.no/mynter/roman.html

2. Pagan Mythology: http://odin..nls.no/viking/e/ewww.htm

3. Ancient Medicine (Note: these sites should be used cautiously if students are not mature enough to handle their contents.)

   http://pacs.unica.it/storia.htm

   http://www.emory.edu/MEDWEB/keyword/history.html

   http://www.medguide.net/

   http://www.perseus.tufts.edu   (Greek Medicine)

   http://indy.radiology.uiowa.edu/   (Greco-Roman Medicine)

4. Archaeoastronomy (the study of astronomical practices related to various mythologies, religion, world views, etc.)

   http://www.wam.umd.edu/~tlalock/archastro/cfaar_as.html

Activity Sheet AW-3 :

INVESTIGATING THE ANCIENT WORLD

Name _____

Using information gathered from these Web sites: http://www.usd.edu/anth/midarch/arch.html, http://www.nhm.ac.uk/index.html, http://rome.classics.lsa.umich.edu, complete items 1–4 below. Then in small groups, do the activity at the bottom.

1. There are certain ways in which archaeologists investigate ancient world sites. One way is to look for pieces of ancient artifacts or other utensils. What are some advantages and disadvantages of different types of artifacts for providing information regarding the civilizations represented by these items?

    _____

    _____

2. What are some other information sources that archaeologists use? What do you consider to be the best sources of information about the Ancient World?

    _____

    _____

3. How did most of the major archeological information we currently know about get discovered?

    _____

    _____

4. How have improvements in modern technology (e.g. x-ray imaging, carbon-dating, etc.) helped us to expand our knowledge of the ancient world?

    _____

    _____

Activity:

Imagine you are visiting another country and you hear an announcement stating that a construction crew has just unearthed what looks like some sort of ancient temple. In a conversation with your traveling companions, the question is asked—"Why excavate?" Discuss in small groups first and then give reasons for and against excavation of the archaeological site.

Activity Sheet AW-4:

LEARN ABOUT ANCIENT ARCHITECTURE

Name _____

The ancient Greeks and Romans were responsible for some of the major developments in architecture. The Greeks contributed the idea of the *Golden Mean* and column construction. Some examples of classical Greek Architecture are The Parthenon, Apollo's Hall, and The British Museum in London, England.

Use information gathered from Web Site http://www.nhm.ac.uk/index.html

1. What is the *Golden Mean* ?

   _____

   _____

   _____

2. How does the Golden Mean affect architecture in general and Greek Architecture in particular?

   _____

   _____

   _____

   _____

3. What other construction advances were made by the Greeks?

   _____

   _____

   _____

   _____

4. What other architectural styles were developed by the Greeks?

   _____

   _____

   _____

ANCIENT EGYPT

Egypt, the gift of the Nile, was a part of the earliest beginnings of civilization, going back to 5000 B.C. Like narrow green ribbons, the river-fed valleys were filled with gardens and fields and surrounded on both sides by high granite cliffs, and sandy plateaus. Deserts stretched into the barren wastes of the vast Sahara, broken only by occasional fertile green patches, called oases. The tributaries to the Nile River made the soil black and rich. They flooded yearly, sometimes even changing course, but always left vast marshes of fertile soil behind. The ancient ones called their land Kemet, meaning black, like their land.

Families and clans learned early to work together to build wall-like dikes, drainage ditches, and irrigation canals in an attempt to tame the river and be able to exist in this region. The engineering and digging of the canals and ditches accomplished three important things:

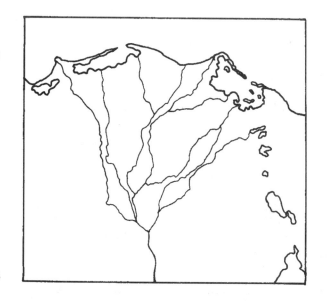

- It drained the swamps.

- It controlled the annual floods.

- It provided a network of swift, smooth water ways, enabling boats to carry people and goods long before wide roads existed on land.

Archaeologists have unearthed evidence that the ancient Egyptians led exciting, eventful, colorful lives. The dry air and ever-drifting sands preserved many of the artifacts and records of ancient Egypt until recent years. For untold centuries, from 5000 B.C. forward, the desert sands gradually and continually buried many villages and towns, tombs and temples.

Egypt is important since it influenced later civilizations in the Mediterranean region, including those of Greece and Rome. Much of our modern knowledge, belief systems and ideals also originated in Egypt. Here we find the world's first national government, a religion that accepted gods and life after death matter-of-factly, and extraordinary feats of architecture and engineering. The ancient Egyptians were creative artists, skilled craftsmen, and adventurous explorers. They had a lively sense of humor, expressing themselves through art and literature. They were the creators of a picture-language, called hieroglyhphics, and the first material for writing, papyrus. They developed a 365-day year and introduced basic geometry and surgery. And yet they considered other peoples to be savages to be captured and enslaved.

MESOPOTAMIA

Mesopotamia—a name that means "The Land Between the Two Rivers"—is another green strip along the Tigris and Euphrates Rivers to the east of Egypt. In Bible times, Mesopotamia was the "Fertile Crescent." It was a long and, in some places, broad band of fertile land, bordered on the west by Persia, to the north by Assyria, and to the east, by Syria and the Arabian Desert. In some places the line between fertile ground and desert was so sharp that one step separated the rich, black, life-giving earth from the dry, dead sand.

The earliest people of the river civilizations led hard lives as nomads, moving about the Fertile Crescent, camping near water points. After centuries of contending with the annual, seasonal flooding of the rivers, they began to work together to build and keep in good repair an irrigation system of banks and canals. As a result of this early ingenuity, their harvests of crops became so plentiful that the people would stockpile surplus food in *store cities* for the drought years they knew would come periodically. Goods were exchanged with foreign traders for fragrant woods, spices, jewels, metal spears and swords. Whenever it became known that the river people were prospering, invaders began attacking. These invaders were mostly poor, hungry nomads from the surrounding hills and countrysides. These wars among neighbors left the canals and the flood walls crumbled. The floods returned. The victors moved in, restored the irrigations systems and the cycle began again.

As clans slowly grouped themselves together, cities began to sprout up along the crescent—Ur of the Chaldeans, Eridu, Erech, Babylon, Mari, Nineveh, Carchemish. Over time, their rulers became more powerful, and they began to make both peace and war with each other. The cities and the green fingers of the Fertile Crescent became the route through Syria and Palestine, connecting Mesopotamia with Egypt.

Ancient traditional stories of this land were passed down by word-of-mouth around campfires. One story was about a Great Flood, and a man who survived it, who was called by different names like Ut-napishtim and Noah. Another was a persistent story of the Tower of Babel. It was about the Sumerians, perhaps the earliest civilization on earth. The people of Sumer lived in Babylonia and the lower Euphrates valley. They were known for building high towers, called *ziggurats,* for their religious ceremonies. These towers were usually square or rectangular, made by piling clay bricks seven stories high. Around them, a ramp-like staircase wound up and around to the top.

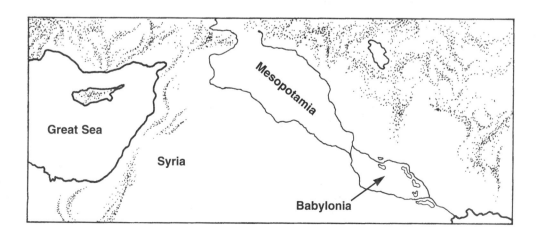

LESSON 7

ANCIENT RIVER CIVILIZATIONS

Egypt is an example of one of the great "River Civilizations" that appeared in the Middle Eastern region around 3000 B.C. Others were Persia, Arabia, Syria, Sumer, and Babylon. Since we have no written records from this time, we are left to speculate as to the reasons why these civilizations appeared at this particular time and in this particular place. Since proximity to rivers played a large role in the development of these communities, it is important to ask some questions about the influence of the rivers on the development of these ancient civilations. Because we do not have written information, we are forced to make theories or hypotheses about how these civilizations were started.

Materials: Copies of the hypotheses below

Web Sites: None unless students choose to search on their own

Teaching the lesson:

Based upon their knowledge of the ancient cultures, direct students to discuss in small groups which of the following hypotheses would most likely explain the growth of River Civilizations. They can make their speculations on Activity Sheet E-1: *The Growth of River Civilizations.*

Hypotheses:

1. The annual flooding deposited a layer of silt, enriching the soil and making it suitable for farming. This rich soil was able to support large numbers of people in a small area. Even in dry years the river valley was attractive to people because of the availability of water for irrigation.

2. The growing of wheat and barley was possible because of the reliable water supply. These grains could be stored for use by towns or villages on the riverbank. This left leisure-time for other activities, such as building houses.

3. The surplus food supply meant that people could specialize in jobs, such as building, copper smithing, or trading. In this way, stable villages and towns grew up around these markets and craft centers. It was no longer necessary for everyone to be involved in hunting or farming.

4. Annual flooding and irrigation required large-scale cooperation and direction. From this need, larger communities developed. These groups created leaders and a form of government. The pharaohs of Egypt probably began as such leaders.

5. Settlements along rivers were more likely to be open to new ideas and techniques from other communities farther along the river. The river was a highway for the spread of new ideas.

6. A chance invention or discovery (e.g. irrigation wheel, grinding stone) could have dramatically increased food production, thus making larger settlements possible.

Extended Activities:

1. Have students compare and create ancient and modern maps of the area of the river civilizations, listing both the old and the new names to connect our study to what is happening in today's news. Ask students to discuss some of the things that seem to have changed little over the centuries.

Activity Sheet E-1:

THE GROWTH OF RIVER CIVILIZATIONS

Name _____

Gather information from the following Web site to complete questions 1 through 4 below:

http://www.clpgh.org/cmnh/tours/egypt/guide.html

1. What role did the annual flooding of the Nile play in the development of an agricultural society? _____

    _____

    _____

2. How was the ancient Egyptian's life affected by the existence of a stable food supply? __

    _____

    _____

    _____

3. What conditions are necessary for the creation of larger settlements?_____

    _____

    _____

    _____

4. Why did the Pharaohs feel it necessary to build the pyramids? Did the Nile have any influence on how and when the pyramids were built?_____

    _____

    _____

    _____

LESSON 8

THE CULTURE OF ANCIENT EGYPT

Provide your students with an overview of ancient Egyptian culture and daily life.

Materials: Activity Sheet E-2: *The Gods of Ancient Egypt*

Web Sites: http://www.sptimes.com/egypt/EgyptCredit.4.2.htm
http://www.memst.edu/egypt/main.html
http://mfah.org/splendor/docs/highlts/
http://www.chron.com/voyager/magazine/97belize/index.html
http://www.mtlake.com/cyberkids/Issue/Legend.html
For information on Mummies:
http://cyberkids.ccsd.k12.wy.us/Conestoga/cruseold.html
Encyclopedia Smithsonian: Egyptian Mummies
http://www.si.edu/welcome/faq/mummies.htm

Teaching the Lesson:

1. The information which can be found at the first site given above is a series of short synopses covering such topics as family life, marriage, food and cooking, cosmetics, hair, jewelry, clothing, housing and furniture, entertainment, art, literature, religion, and government.

2. After students have read through these brief introductions, have them form groups of three or four (depending on class size) and choose a topic they can research in greater detail. They will present their findings to the class. If there are not enough topics, have them log on to another site where they can find additional topics to explore.

3. The gods of Ancient Egypt were an important part of an Egyptian's daily life and were celebrated by a number of religious gatherings and feasts throughout the year. Parents often used the gods in children's stories to reinforce moral teachings. Many Egyptian gods took human form and had children by the pharaohs, who then claimed to be a son or daughter of the "god." Since animals played a large part in the Egyptians' daily lives, it is not surprising that many Egyptian gods were a combination of animal and human forms.

4. Do a search on "Egyptian Gods." Then complete the Activity Sheet E-2: *The Gods of Ancient Egypt.*

Extended Activities:

When you have finished doing the readings and exploring the sites online, go to the http://www.si.edu/welcome/faq/mummies.htm site where you will find a Pyramid Crossword puzzle that you can complete to test your knowledge of Ancient Egypt.

Activity Sheet E-2:

THE GODS OF ANCIENT EGYPT

Name _____

A good starting point is the Ancient Egypt section of the Times Launch Point

    Web site at: http://www.latimes.com/launchpoint/

To increase your knowledge of Egyptian gods, first do a search on the Internet for the gods listed below. Then answer the questions and fill in the chart with the appropriate information.

1. Since the Egyptians were strong believers in judgment after death and an afterlife, which of their gods helped them make the transition to the afterlife? _____

    _____

    _____

    _____

2. What is the relationship between the role the god played in Egyptian culture and/or religion and the attributes of the particular animal from which the god took its form? _____

    _____

    _____

    _____

3. The main Egyptian gods are given below. Use a search engine of your choice to find out more information about each of these gods. Fill in the chart with your findings.

Name	Job/Role	Physical Appearance	Level of Importance
Re			
Osiris			
Isis			
Horus			
Anubis			
Thoth			

LESSON 9

TOURING THE PYRAMIDS

Help your students locate the ancient pyramids and gather some necessary information about their construction and uses.

Materials: Activity Sheet E-3: *Locate the Pyramids*

Web Sites: http://www.memst.edu/egypt/main.html
http://www-lib.haifa.ac.il/www/art/archimedia.html
http://www.dia.org/galleries/ancient/egypt/egypt.html

Teaching the Lesson:

1. During a 500 year period from 2700-2200 B.C., the all-powerful rulers began the *Age of the Pyramids*. On the very edge of the desert, the Egyptians began to build huge burial tombs, called pyramids, for their rulers who were known as pharaohs. Over 20 major pyramids would reveal mysterious bits and pieces of an ancient civilization which was seeking answers to questions about man and society, nature, and God. Out of one giant section of solid rock was carved the Great Sphinx near the Great Pyramid of Giza (Al Jizah).

2. Ask students to log on to the University of Memphis site, http://www.menst.edu/egypt/main.html

3. Have students choose the Color Tour of Egypt

4. Allow students to visit the major pyramids including Giza, Aswan, and Abu Simbel, as well as other major temples and modern sites.

5. Have students answer the questions on Activity Sheet E-3: *Locate the Pyramids.*

Extended Activities:

1. After reading through the first site listed above for information on the Pyramids, as a class, discuss how the pyramids might be have been built. Have students create a project that will show a possible method of construction of the pyramids or the Great Sphinx.

2. Have students make a picture or model of what they think the inside of a pharaoh's tomb might look like. Label the things we might find there.

3. Have students draw a map of Egypt labeling the locations of the major pyramids, as well as other sites they consider to be among the most important of their study of Egypt.

Activity Sheet E-3:

LOCATE THE PYRAMIDS

Name _____

A few excellent online sites for you to visit are:

Guardian's Meidum Home Page   http://guardians.net/egypt/
The Great Temple of Abu Simbel   http://www.ccer.ggl.ruu.nl/abu_simbel/abu_simbel1.html
Treasures of Tutankhamum   http://wkweb4.cableinet.co.uk/iwhawkins/egypt/
Akhet Egyptology   http:/wkweb4.cableinet.co.yk/iwhawkings/Egypt

1. Consider some of the mysteries of the pyramids that may never be solved because written records are lacking and so is a strong oral tradition. Consequently, we are forced to hypothesize as to the meaning and purpose the pyramids represent. The three primary mysteries are:

   • the accuracy of the buildings themselves. The walls are almost perfect even though they rise over 400 feet in the air.

   • the way that the huge stones were moved from one place to another. Some of the stones are of local origin, while others appear to come from Aswan which is upriver from the site. How did they get there? It is well known that the early Egyptians did not use horses or wheeled wagons.

   • the construction details of the building. For instance, joints were accurate to one millimeter. (Modern stone masons usually use 15-20 mm of mortar.) There is also the question of how the sarcophagus got into the tomb. It is 5 cm (about 2 inches) wider than the tunnel that leads into the burial room.

2. Do a search to find the exact details archaeologists know about how the pyramids were built.

3. On the back of this sheet, for each one of the "mysteries" given above, formulate three hypotheses and/or explanations that you think are reasonable in terms of explaining the "mystery." Discuss your ideas with members of your group or with the rest of the class. Come to some agreement as to which might be the most reasonable.

4. Incorporate your information about pyramid building by designing a pyramid showing its chambers, tunnels, and a "dummy" entrance (to trick possible tomb robbers).

5. Describe who the builders of the pyramids were. _____

_____

6. What was the purpose for building the pyramids? _____

_____

7. Why do you think pyramids were built using the triangle as the main shape? _____

_____

_____

Activity Sheet   E-4:

USING EGYPTIAN HIEROGLYPHICS

Name _____

A	A	B	C/K	D
E/I/Y	F/V	G	H	H
I/Y/E	J	L	M	M
N	N	O/U/W	P	Q
R	S/Z	SH/CH	T	TH
U/W/O	X	Y/E/I	Z/S	

One of the most famous achievements of the ancient Egyptians was the creation of hieroglyphics. For many years, the meaning of the strange symbols was not known. Then the Rosetta Stone was discovered in Western Egypt in July of 1799. It contained a single text with three translations, one in Egyptian hieroglyphics, one in Demotic (a simplified hieroglyphics system), and one in Greek (a known language). This allowed the text to be translated and meaning assigned to the hieroglyphics. In 1801, when Cairo was threatened by war, Sir Ralph Abercromby brought the Rosetta Stone to England. It is now located in the British Museum in London, England.

Activity Sheet E-4:

USING EGYPTIAN HIEROGLYPHICS *(cont.)*

Name _____

Hieroglyphics do not have a one-to-one correspondence to sounds like the letters of our alphabet. This means that the writer must help the reader along by choosing the appropriate hieroglyphics.

1. Study the chart of sounds and representative symbols on the previous page. For specific information on the Rosetta Stone, go to the Cleveland Museum of Art web site below. Use a dictionary to look up words you do not know.

   http://www.clemusart.com/archive/pharaoh/rosetta/

   Other interesting Web sites:
   http://www.cultures.com/meso/
   http://www.mesoweb.com/welcome.html
   http://www.mesoweb.com/encyc/encyc/index.html

2. Study a short tutorial found in the following Web site to complete the activities below:

   http://www.torstar.com/rom/egypt/#cartouche"

3. Define hieroglyphics. _____

   _____

4. Write your name(s) in hieroglyphics. Make modifications as needed to help the reader.

   _____

   _____

   _____

5. Write four phrases in hieroglyphics. Again, consider what modifications are necessary.

   _____

   _____

   _____

THE ANCIENT ROMAN EMPIRE

After the Greeks, all roads led to the Roman Empire from about 753 B.C. to A.D. 476. Though the boundaries changed many times during its 1300-year history, at the height of its power and size, around A.D. 117, the Roman Empire circled the Mediterranean Sea. It took in the northern coast of Africa, the eastern coast of Asia Minor, plus most of Mesopotamia, going from the Persian Gulf and the Red Sea up through most of Europe all the way to northern Britain and east to Hispania.

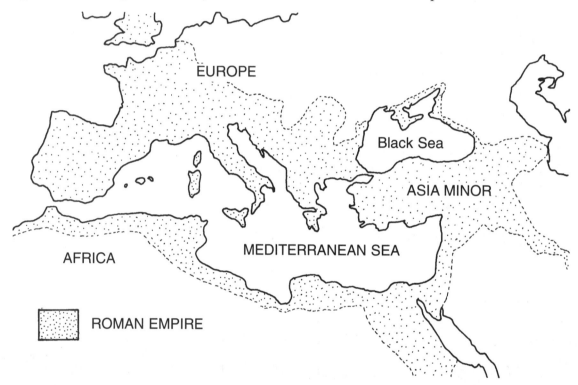

It is hard to describe the "average Roman" of that time. Cultured Arabs, Jewish scholars, Egyptian farmers, and barbaric Germanic tribesmen continued to lead the lives of their ancient ancestors. The Roman way of life included millions of people who spoke various languages, embraced their own traditions, and worshiped different gods. Their unity however came from the military power and government that grew out of the city of Rome which became the capital of a huge empire.

Rome was for centuries the center of the known world. As such, the Romans set up a strong government and provided leadership in architecture and the arts. The Romans built elaborate houses, bridges, and roads, some of which can still be seen today. They developed the first super highway system when it was necessary for soldiers and traders to move quickly from one part of the empire to another. They constructed large arenas where the people could bet on their favorite charioteer and amphitheaters where the entertainment consisted of cheering on the battling gladiators or the condemned criminals and Christians being thrown to wild animals. Much time was spent in huge establishments with pools, hot and cold baths, along with gymnasiums, art galleries, and libraries.

LESSON 10

INTRODUCTION TO THE ROMAN EMPIRE

Introduce your students to the ancient Roman culture by showing the day-to-day living habits of the Romans.

Materials: Activity Sheet RE-1: Everyday Life in Roman Times

Web Sites: Ancient Roman Dishes (food)
http://www.mit.edu:8001/people/wchuang/cooking/recipes/Roman/Ancient_Roman.html
Ancient Art of Rome
http://www.dia.org/galleries/ancient/rome/rome.html
A Collection of Resources on the Roman Empire
http://ireland.iol.ie/~coolmine/typ/romans/intro.html
General History/Byzantine Empire
http://history.hanover.edu/medieval/byzantine.htm
The Hunterian Museum:The Romans in Scotland
http://www.gla.ac.uk:80/Museum/HuntMus/romans/
Byzantine History Opening Page
http://www.serve.com/byzance/#Top

Teaching the Lesson:

1. Introduce the study of the Roman Empire with the brief overview.
2. Allow ample time for students to search the web to learn about a typical Roman day.
3. Use Activity Sheet RE-1: *Everyday Life in Roman Times* to chart information.
4. Have each student choose a topic of particular interest to do further research individually, using keyword skills to find new web sites. Students can report findings back to the class.

Extended Activities:

1. Map-makers can search out and create maps for significant geographic locations of that time, showing how extensive the Roman Empire was, and using the ancient and modern names. A map of historic places in the old city of Rome could include symbols for the events that took place there. Names written in green would indicate sites that still exist.

2. Pompeii was destroyed when Mt. Vesuvius erupted without warning in 79 A.D., "freezing" everything exactly as it was at the time of the eruption. It left a wealth of prevolcanic artifacts, all preserved in excellent condition. Have students discuss and/or make some of the unearthed items. What might the most important findings have been?

3. Ask students to create a play about the activities of one family on the day Mt. Vesuvius erupted.

4. Allow students to log on to Roman feasts and festivals, (the first site listed) and search, plan, and serve a Roman feast, complete with togas and traditional foods. Share legendary stories of Rome's beginnings, such as The *Fall of Troy*, *Romulus and Remus*, and the Roman gods and goddesses.

Activity Sheet RE-1:

EVERYDAY LIFE IN ROMAN TIMES

Name _____

Do a search on the Internet to learn about daily life in ancient Rome.

Area of Life	Poor Farmers	City Dwellers	Wealthy Class
Daily Work			
Shelter			
Clothing			
Transportation			
Amusements			

LESSON 11

ROMAN GODS AND GODDESSES

Allow your students to discover that the Roman family tree of gods and goddesses was very similar to that of ancient Greece. Often only the names were changed.

Materials: Activity Sheet RE-2: *Family Tree of Ancient Gods*

Web Sites: http:www.vaction.net.gr/p/mithos.html

students use their keyword searching skills to locate other sites

Teaching the Lesson:

1. Roman gods and goddesses were similar to those from ancient Greece. In fact, in some cases, only the names were changed.

2. Assign Activity Sheet RE-2: *Family Tree of Ancient Gods* for students to describe some of the major Roman gods and goddesses before making a family tree showing relationships.

3. Have students write in the names of the equivalent Greek gods in parentheses.

Extended Activities:

1. Have students search for some of the most famous stories of the Roman gods and goddesses and share their findings with the class in the form of readings, Reader's Theater, or simple plays.

2. Have students create easy-to-read collections of stories about the Greek and Roman gods and goddesses designed for younger readers, complete with illustrations. Ask the students' permission to share their collections with younger classes, or put them on tape for early-grade centers.

3. Have students create two-sided posters for each of the most important Roman Gods that have a Greek equivalent, Roman on one side, Greek on the other, or side by side.

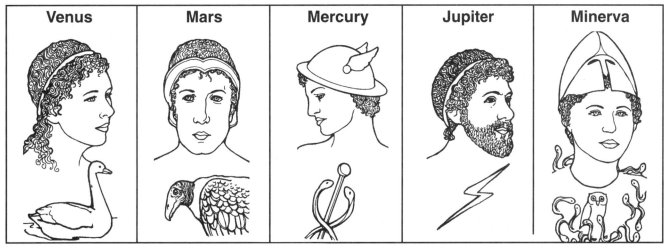

Venus | Mars | Mercury | Jupiter | Minerva

Activity Sheet RE-2:

FAMILY TREE OF ANCIENT GODS

Name _____

Use keywords to search for information to complete the chart below. On the back make a family tree showing the relationship between the Roman gods and goddesses. For those who have a Greek equivalent, put the Greek name in parentheses below the Roman name.

Roman Name	Title	Greek Name	Powers
Mercury			
Mars			
Venus			
Minerva			
Jupiter			

LESSON 12

ROMAN MOSAICS

Show your students examples of Roman Mosaics which embodied principles of geometry while serving an aesthetic and functional purpose.

Materials: Activity Sheet RE-3: *Create Your Own Roman Mosaic*

Web Sites: http://www.umich.edu/~kelseydb/Exhibits/WondrousGlass/glass.html
                   http://www.umich.edu/~pfoss/ROMARCH.html
                   http://206.151.74.156 pompeii/images.htm

Teaching the Lesson:

1. Many Roman homes had mosaic floors and wall coverings. The most commonly used patterns were geometric ones which were based on a square. When the influence of Rome extended to other locations, Roman mosaics were incorporated into new buildings. In particular, there are a large number of mosaic floors and walls in Britain. Good sites for examples of Roman mosaics are listed above.

2. One of the ways we can establish that the Romans lived in England is by finding houses which have mosaics as floor and wall coverings.

3. Geometric shapes and patterns were used as borders around the main mosaic pattern. Students should notice that many times the patterns are repetitive, thereby creating a very effective border.

4. Have students visit some of the Roman web sites above to find the kinds of ornamentation and decoration that were used in the Roman-built houses and villas. Have students locate some other mosaics left by the Romans, and download or print out the images to show to the class.   (Refer to Appendices A & B to learn how to do this with your browser).

5. Roman houses were built in certain shapes. Have students draw a floor plan, front and inside-view, of a typical Roman city-dwelling. Have students explain why the dwelling was built in its particular way. Did the building style change according to the climate and location?

Extended Activities :

1. Have students draw a few Roman mosaic border patterns, then use one to outline something they have created for this unit of study.

2. Expand on #5 above by having students draw additional floor plans, front and side views, for the houses of the very poor Roman farmer and the very wealthy nobleman.

3. Have students cite some instances of Roman influence on architecture in the different regions conquered by the Roman army.

CREATE YOUR OWN ROMAN MOSAIC

Name _____

　　　72

LESSON 13

THE ROMAN FORM OF GOVERNMENT

Introduce your students to one of the oldest examples of an organized form of government.

Materials: Activity Sheet RE-4: *Structure of the Roman Government*

Web Sites: The Hunterian Museum: The Romans in Scotland
http://www.gla.ac.uk:80/Museum/HuntMus/romans/Index.html

Byzantine History Opening Page
http://www.serve.com/byzance/#Top

Preparation: Students should have some knowledge of the Roman Empire and our own governmental system of democracy.

Teaching the Lesson:

The Roman form of government was based loosely upon that used by the Greeks and other civilizations located in the Mediterranean regions.

1. Have students begin by doing a search on "Ancient Rome Government."

2. Have students check the rankings to see which ones contain all three keywords.

3. Have students select a site that appears to have the information they need, and log on to that site. (If it is not available, have them go to the next site on their list.)

4. Have students keep searching the sources until you find one which has the answers to the questions on the Activity Sheeet R-4: *Structure of the Roman Government.*

Extended Activities:

1. Have students search out information on the Senate, the *Comitia Curiata,* the *Forum,* and the *Pax Romana.* Choose a creative way of reporting to the class whatever information they found.

2. After students have established the form of government for Ancient Rome, have them investigate some other civilizations, past and present, to determine what form of government they established. Have students categorize those they find by the civilization's form of government.

3. Have students select three to five countries in the world today which have unstable governments. Ask students what form of government those countries are using? Have students discuss in small groups why they think the form of government for each of these countries is not working well.

4. Ask students if they could improve our American form of democracy, how would they change it? How would they go about making sure these changes are put into effect? Have students write a letter to the appropriate Congressperson with the suggestion they feel would be most effective.

Activity Sheet RE-4:

THE STRUCTURE OF THE ROMAN GOVERNMENT

Name _____

Do a search on "Ancient Rome Government" looking for sites that contain all three words.

Using Web site information, fill in the chart below to show the similarities and differences between Rome's form of government and a modern democracy.

GOVERNMENT OF ROME   **MODERN DEMOCRACY**

_____

_____

_____

The following people and/or groups of people made up the Roman government. Define the role of each in the government structure.

plebians _____

patricians _____

consuls _____

pro-consuls _____

praetors _____

tribunes _____

quaestor _____

pontifex _____

censor _____

Activity Sheet RE-4:

THE STRUCTURE OF THE ROMAN GOVERNMENT *(cont.)*

Name _____

Do a search for Web sites that contain the information:

1. What role did the Pope take during Roman/Christian times?

   _____

   _____

2. Choose two famous Roman Emperors and provide a brief description of their reign.

   _____

   _____

3. The Roman Army was one of the best in the world at one time. Choose one of the topics below to investigate further the influence that this army had on the advancement of civilization.

   • Julius Caesar, a great general and Roman Emperor _____

   _____

   _____

   • Hadrian's Wall and the Romans in Great Britain _____

   _____

   _____

   • The "Gladiator Entertainment" in Rome _____

   _____

   _____

   • The building of roads and bridges that were used by the Roman Army _____

   _____

   _____

4. What brought about the fall of the Roman Empire?_____

   _____

ANCIENT GREECE

Greece has been called "the birthplace of Western Civilization." It is the place where the concept of a democracy originated—the idea that every citizen should take an active part in the government. Over 2000 years ago, it began as a small kingdom but it controlled much of the area bordering the Mediterranean and Black Seas. Herodotus, a historian, once wrote, "In Greece, poverty is always a guest." Farm and city folk alike led hard but simple lives, working from sunup to sundown. The plains people and the island people each created their own city-states which quarreled and fought over the scarcity of land. Two of the most important city-states were Athens and Sparta.

Ancient Greece was far more advanced than any previous civilization. The ancient Greeks were the first people to study geometry, botany, zoology, physics, political theory, and medicine. The world's first poets, orators, dramatists, historians, and philosophers, were Greek. The Greeks were skilled in music, architecture, sculpting, and painting, and made important contributions to the development of written communication. Historians agree that literature was the Greeks' single most important contribution to western civilization.

The Greek gods were not the dark, fearful idols of their neighbors. They were superhuman beings who looked and acted much like humans, except they were seen as taller, more powerful, more beautiful or handsome than any mortal could be. They could do no wrong. These radiant gods lived on top of Mt. Olympus, a mountain much too high for mere man to ascend. The gods, however, sometimes chose to come down to Earth, both as themselves or in the form of animals or human beings. The major gods were: Zeus (the king), and Hera (his wife), Apollo, Dionysus, Hades, Hephaestus, Hermes, Poseidon, Aphrodite, Artemis, and Demeter. The legends of the gods and goddesses were filled with fire-breathing monsters and multi-headed beasts to be slain.

The Greeks built cities of temples, treasure-houses, and special buildings to honor their gods. They enjoyed elaborate feasts and festivals which included prayers, animal sacrifices, dramas, and athletic contests. We have the Greeks to thank for starting the Olympic games which continue to influence modern day sports and athletes internationally.

Magnificent ruins from the ancient times remain to hint at the glory of their gods and their past achievements: the road at Corinth, the Theater at Dodone, Agora in Athens, the Guardian Lions on Delos, the Parthenon in Athens, the Palace at Knossos, the Temple of Apollo at Delphi, and the Temple of Athena Lindia at Knidos.

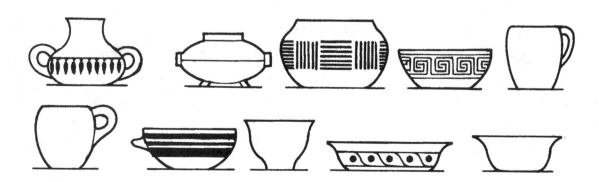

LESSON 14

INTRODUCTION TO ANCIENT GREECE

Give your students a "feel" for what it was like to live in ancient Greece.

Materials: Activity Sheet G-1: *Everyday Life in Ancient Greece*
                 Activity Sheet G-2: *Women in Ancient Greece*

Web Sites: http://www.museum.upenn.edu/Greek_World/Intro.htm
                 http://info.desy.de/gna/interpedia/greek_myth/greek_myth.html

Teaching the Lesson:

1. The importance of ancient Greece to the development of modern civilization is well-documented. However, less emphasis has been placed on the everyday life of Ancient Greek citizens. One of the best ways of finding out about a culture is to read about their mythology and other fruits of their imagination. Have students log on to the excellent sites above and explore the topic of their choice:

The Place of the Home	Marriage and Death
The Role of Women	Games and Festivals
Clothing and Dress	Work and Slavery
Jewelry and Decoration	Greek Mythology

2. Have students record their findings under the appropriate category on Activity Sheet G-1: *Everyday Life in Ancient Greece* and Activity Sheet G-2: *Women in Ancient Greece.*

Extended Activities:

In spite of the fact that the Ancient Greeks and Romans were often at war with their neighbors, somehow they still found time to pursue artistic endeavors. The Romans made beautiful mosaics on the floors and walls of their homes while the Greeks made exquisite pottery and sculptures.

1. Students can use keywords to search for the various types of Greek pottery until they find one design that could be used to make their own pottery.

2. Have students investigate Greek sculpture and Greek gods to find a piece of sculpture they can reproduce. Write up a title and description on a small index card to display with it.

3. Many of the descriptions and functions of the Roman gods and goddesses came directly from the Greek gods. Ask students to choose one or two gods and verbally compare the Roman and Greek versions.

Activity Sheet G-1:

EVERYDAY LIFE IN ANCIENT GREECE

Name _____

http://www.museum.upenn.edu/Greek_World/Intro.html

Use the above Web site to search for information about everyday life in Ancient Greece, starting with the topics below. Write brief notes about what you find on each subject.

The Place of the Home _____

_____

The Role of Women _____

_____

Clothing and Dress_____

_____

Jewelry and Decoration _____

_____

Marriage and Death _____

_____

Games and Festivals _____

_____

Work and Slavery_____

_____

Greek Mythology _____

_____

Activity Sheet G-2:

WOMEN IN ANCIENT GREECE

Name _____

Gather information from Web Site http://www.museum.upenn.edu/Greek_World/Intro.htm
to complete the following questions.

1. What was the role of women in ancient Greece? _____

_____

_____

_____

2. Were there any exceptions to this role? _____

_____

_____

_____

3. Explain women's citizenship rights in Ancient Greece? _____

_____

_____

_____

4. What did women do in the Olympic Games? Could they compete? _____

_____

_____

_____

5. When theater became prominent in Greek society, how did that alter the status of
   women? _____

_____

_____

LESSON 15

GAMES OF THE ANCIENT OLYMPICS

Introduce your students to the Games of the Ancient Olympics—the history, the contests, and their cultural impact.

Materials: Activity Sheet G-3: *The Original Olympics Games*
Activity Sheet G-4: *The First Olympic Events*

Web Sites: http://devlab.dartmouth.edu/olympic/Games
http://olympics.tufts.edu/culture
http://www.forthnet.gr/olympics/
http://www.nbc4dc.com/olympic/history.html
http://www.com-stock.com/dave/olysymb.htm

Teaching the Lesson:

1. One of the most important contributions of the Ancient Greeks to civilization was the starting of the original Olympic Games. These games ran from 776 B.C. to 195 A.D. and attracted participants and spectators from all over the Greek World. On the surface, the games were an athletic contest. Actually, however, it is important to point out that they were held in honor of the highest ranking god, Zeus. During the time of the games (approximately one month), participants were not allowed to take up arms against one another.

2. Have students choose one of the sites listed above and explore some aspect of the games that interests them.

3. After reading information from several sites, have students answer the questions on Activity Sheet G-3: *The Original Olympic Games.*

4. As the games continued, events were added. Some had unusual names. Have students identify the events and complete the chart with dates and a brief description on Activity Sheet G-4: *The Original Olympic Events.*

Extended Activity:

1. When Activity Sheet G-4 is completed, have students design Olympic symbols for the ancient events, much like those used in our modern Olympics.

2. Have each student create an Olympic event at which they believe they excel. Let their imaginations run and keep it fun. Perhaps they can make a small book of Class Olympic Winners and make small medals for each category.

Activity Sheet G-3:

THE ORIGINAL OLYMPIC GAMES

Name _____

Gather information from Web Sites below to complete numbers 1-5.

http://devlab.dartmouth.edu/olympic/games
http://olympics.tufts.edu/culture.html
http://www.forthnet.gr/olympics/
http://www.nbc4dc.com/olympic/history.html

1. Why were the games originally called the "Olympic" games? _____

_____

2. Identify the five events that were part of the original pentathlon. _____

_____

3. In modern times, the pentathlon has been replaced by the decathlon. How many events are in this activity? _____

_____

4. How did the Marathon race get its name? _____

_____

5. Why were women excluded from the games?_____

_____

Because the games were of cultural as well as sporting value, their contributions to the overall culture were lasting. To answer the following questions, log on to the site shown below:

http://olympics.tufts.edu/culture.html

1. List and describe some possible cultural outcomes of the Olympic Games._____ _____

_____

2. What other benefits have been attributed to the games throughout the years? _____

_____

Activity Sheet G-4:

THE FIRST OLYMPIC EVENTS

Name _____

Some of the first Olympic games had unusual names. Search online to identify the events below and write a short description of each.

NAME OF EVENT	STARTING/ENDING	DESCRIPTION
Stade-race		
Diaulos		
Dolichos		
Pentathlon		
Boxing		
Wrestling		
Tethrippon		
Pankration		
Apene or anabates		
Calpe		
Synoris		
Chariot racing		

LESSON 16

INTRODUCTION TO GREEK ARCHITECTURE

Show your students examples of ancient and modern Greek Architecture.

Materials: Activity Sheet G-5: *Ancient Architecture*

Web Sites: Ancient City of Athens
                http:/www.indiana.edu/~kglowack/Athens/Athens.html

Cultural Map of Hellas (Greece)
                http://www.culture.gr/2/21/maps/hellas.html

Mycenaean Palace
                http://www-lib.haifa.ac.il/www/art/Mycenaen.html

Ancient Greece, Unplugged!
                http://oakview.fcps.edu:80/~smith/greece/

Preparation: Students should have been given a general introduction to Ancient Greece, its cities and its basic architectural styles.

Teaching the Lesson:

1. The three styles of columns used by the ancient Greeks were Doric, Ionic, and Corinthian. Have students search online to find samples of these three columns and draw pictures of them on the back of Activity Sheet G-5: *Ancient Architecture.*

2. In your state (or province), many of the government buildings will show the influence of Greek architecture. See if you can find three buildings which fit the Greek model and draw sketches of them above. For each building indicate which style of column is used: Ionic, Doric, or Corinthian.

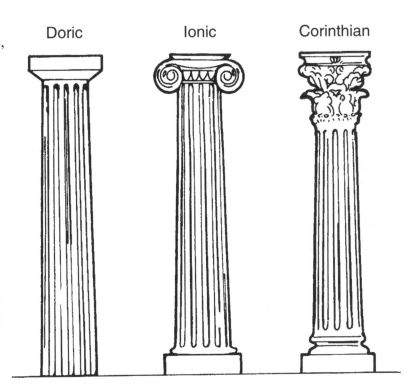

Doric   Ionic   Corinthian

Activity Sheet G-5:

ANCIENT ARCHITECTURE

Name _____

We are constantly being shown images of famous buildings in other locations throughout the world. In many instances, what we see are Greek influences. After looking at a number of these buildings, certain aspects become obvious. Consider these questions: Does the building have columns? Has the building been dedicated for a specific civic or religious purpose?

1. Search the Internet to find information about each of the prominent Ancient Greek and Roman buildings listed below.

2. On the chart below, write a short description for each site. Be sure to include the location of the site, the architect, if known, and any other pertinent information. Draw a quick but accurate sketch of the building and label it.

Greek Buildings	Roman Buildings
The Parthenon	The Colosseum
Temple of Apollo	The Pantheon
Palace of Nestor	St. Peter's of Rome
(Olympia- Temple of Zeus)	The Forum
Acropolis (Athens)	Flavian Palace

3. Research five examples of classical architecture in city and government buildings found in large metropolitan US cities, such as New York, Boston, and Washington, D.C.

4. On another paper, give the location of these five buildings. Describe the features they have that make them qualified to be labeled as good examples of Greek or Roman architecture. Draw and label a sketch of each building you have chosen.

MEDIEVAL TIMES

The Middle Ages, also known as the Medieval Times, extends from the end of the Roman Empire to about 1500 A.D. Historians use 400 A.D. as the starting date, although the demise of the Roman Empire took several hundred years. By then the Empire had become so weak that the German tribes were able to conquer it. The Germanic way of life gradually combined with the Roman way of life to form a civilization which historians call the Medieval Times.

The Romans considered their conquerors to be barbarians, meaning uncivilized. They were, in fact, a rough, warring, ignorant people. They lived in tribes, governed by a chief. The few laws they had were based on superstition. Large, full-bearded, crude in manner, and fierce in appearance, they were brave warriors fighting with spears and shields, dressed in coarse linen and animal skins.

The Germanic laws of superstition replaced the strong Roman system of security and safety that comes from law and order. The barbarian *trial by ordeal* determined guilt or innocence. The accused was required to pick up a red-hot iron with his bare hands or plunge his arm into boiling water. Wounds that healed in three days proved innocence. Unhealed wounds resulted in hanging.

With the barbarians came the power of their armies and less freedom to use the extensive road system the Romans had constructed. This resulted in the loss of trade and communications that the Romans had built up between their thriving cities. Cities began to be divided up into large land *manors* ruled by wealthy landlords and defended by knights in armor. Most of the townspeople moved to the countryside to become peasants under the king's control, farming his fields, caring for his vineyards, performing all the tasks required by his huge holdings and his household, producing all the things his villages needed. The mighty stone castles that were built to defend him also gave protection to his peasants. The royal family, his lords, ladies, and knights feasted in the royal banquet halls, entertained by wandering poets, actors, minstrels, court jesters and jugglers.

Towns were abandoned. They disappeared with the middle class that had produced the trade and industry of the great Roman Empire. As schools and the education systems were forgotten, fewer and fewer people could read and write. Knowledge and skills of the sciences, architecture, and the fine arts, along with the works of the world's first poets, orators, dramatists, historians, and philosophers of the Greek and Roman periods were temporarily lost.

The only civilizing force in the early years of the Middle Ages was the Christian Church. Men began to worship only one god, the same god. Traveling missionaries spread the Christian faith great distances and reintroduced the old Roman concepts of government, citizenship, township, laws, and justice. It was the Church that saved the Western civilization from ignorance through its cathedrals, which were the centers of worship, and through monasteries, which were the communities of monks. These "men of the cloth" served God through their reading and writing of the holy "books" and their prayers. Both the clergy and the monks worked to preserve the valuable ancient scrolls and manuscripts.

By the High Middle Ages (1000-1200 A.D.), the Church had begun to re-establish the school systems in Europe. Towns began to spring up along the main trade routes. Peace and security once again allowed the people to devote themselves to scientific and artistic ideas.

LESSON 17

INTRODUCTION TO MEDIEVAL TIMES

Provide students with information on the everyday life of medieval nobles, peasants, and clergy.

Materials: Activity Sheet MT-1: *Life in Medieval Times*

Web Sites: http://www.castlewales.com/home.html#PleaseSelect

http://www.english-heritage.org.uk/resimedi.htm (for peasants)

http:// sunsite.berkeley.edu/OMACL (Online Medieval and Classical Library)

http://www.pbm.com/~lindahl/food.html

Teaching the Lesson:

1. Have students log on and explore websites above on their own.

2. Show students how to create their own chart of categories on which to record the basics of the information they discover.

3. Have students use Activity Sheet MT-1: *Life in Medieval Times* to check for understanding of some of the key concepts and terms.

4. In pairs or small groups, have students choose a topic of interest to them to research in more depth. Formulate a brief product report and share with the class.

Extended Activities:

1. As with any time period, food played an important role in the day-to-day life of all people. Search the last Web site listed above to discover and write about some of the foods that were popular during medieval times.

2. Allow students to plan and enjoy a small Medieval feast to sample some of the foods of this period.

Activity Sheet MT-1:

EVERYDAY LIFE IN MEDIEVAL TIMES

Name _____

Log on and explore Web sites related to the Middle Ages.

1. How did European life change after the Germanic invasions? _____

   _____

   _____

2. What three social classes emerged during the Middle Ages? _____

   _____

3. What happened to the towns over the long period of the Middle Ages? _____

   _____

   _____

4. What economic and social gains came to a halt in this period? _____

   _____

   _____

5. What effect did the Church have on the Middle Ages? _____

   _____

   _____

6. Define the following key terms:

   • Feudalism _____

   • Black Death _____

   • manor _____

   • vassal _____

   • humanism _____

LESSON 18

MEDIEVAL HERALDRY

Introduce your students to Medieval Heraldry through examining coats of arms and creating a personal shield.

Materials: Activity Sheet M-2: *Make Your Own Heraldry Shield*

Web Site: http://www.digiserv.com/heraldry/referenc.htm

It was at this time that "heraldry" appeared. Heraldry was just another one of the outcomes which appeared as a result of changes to the social structure during the Middle Ages. In this case, the wearing of armor to protect the face also made it impossible to identify the person. This created a need for a quick and easy means of identification which would be unique to the person (or group of people). Sometimes it meant using a shield as a protection during battle. At other times a specific color would be used. The crests, which are still used today, were beneficial for people who are unable to read. As in the Middle Ages, seals of approval were also widespread.

Teaching the Lesson:

1. Have students log on to the Heraldry on the Internet Site above.

2. On the second screen, have students choose "Coat of Arms Search."

3. Have students submit their surname (last name) for a search.

4. If they get a Coat of Arms for their surname, have them print it out and hand it in.

5. To find a coat of arms with labels for all of the appropriate symbols, have students log on to the site: http://www.hookup.net/~dbirk/hb.html

6. If a student doesn't receive a coat of arms, have the computer generate one for that student.

7. Remember that there may be some cost involved. If they are requested to make some form of payment in order to receive a coat of arms, instruct them to contact you before proceeding further.

LESSON 18

MEDIEVAL HERALDRY *(cont.)*

Teaching the Lesson *(cont.)*

8. Once students have logged onto the Heraldry site above, they can view two screens listing the addresses for topics related to Heraldry. Limit their choices to the following categories:

What's Hot
Coat of Arms Search
Computer-Generated
    Coat of Arms
International Heraldic
    Glossary

Heraldry
Order of Chivalry
Heraldic Organizations
National Heraldry
Heraldic Clipart

Coat of Arms
Military
National
Surnames
United States

Related
Surnames
Arms & Armor
Flags
Castles
Maps
Medieval resources
Dictionaries

Heraldry Articles
Heraldry
Notes on Heraldry
Heraldry Lecture
Tools & Techniques of
Genealogical Research
    by Joseph C. Wolf

Extended Activities:

1. Have each student (either alone or in a group) find modern day examples of family Coats of Arms, Seals of Approval, or other identification pieces.

2. Have students investigate the Society for Creative Anachronism (http://www.sca.org) which promotes the continuation of medieval customs and activities by sponsoring contests and reenactments of jousting tournaments.

Activity Sheet M-2:

MAKE YOUR OWN HERALDRY SHIELD

Name _____

Directions for Activity:

1. Log on to the Heraldry site:

   http://www.english-heritage.org.uk/resimedi.htm

2. Using the information from that site, design your own heraldry shield on the outline below.

3. Label each of the symbols you have chosen.

4. Write a brief description of each symbol and its meaning on the back of this sheet.

5. Share the meaning of each of your shield symbols with the rest of the class.

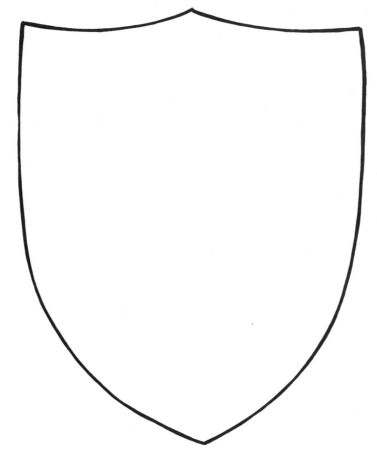

LESSON 19

MEDIEVAL CASTLES

Introduce your students to castles, the living conditions, location, purposes, construction, and function in the community.

Materials: sheet of paper and pencil/pen

Web Sites: Castles on the Web
                    http://fox.nstn.ca/~tmonk/castle/castle.html

                    The Castles of Wales
                    http://www.castlewales.com/home.html#1PleaseSelect

                    Life in a Medieval Castle
                    http://www.castlewales.com/life.html

                    Castle Siegecraft and Defense
                    http://www.castlewales.com/siege.html

Teaching the Lesson:
The Castles on the Web site has several sections which will give students an excellent opportunity to expand their knowledge and vocabulary in reference to all aspects of castle-building, history, and location, including existing castles.

The categories which contain information at this site are:

Introduction	Castles for Kids
Castle Tours	Castle Quest
Castle Collections	Glossary of Castle Terms
Castle Image Archives	Castles of the World

1. Have students log on to the above Web sites to gain general information on castles.

2. Assign small groups of three or four students to choose one of the above topics that interests them to research in greater depth and report to the class. Keep in mind that they can also access other links from this site, do a search to locate other sites, or try some of the sites listed above.

LESSON 19

MEDIEVAL CASTLES *(cont.)*

3. After investigating several sites about castles, in small groups, discuss the answers to the following questions:

   Why did the people of the Middle Ages feel a need to build castles?

   What materials were used to construct castles?

   What defense systems were built into the castles to make it difficult to scale the castle walls?

4. Using Activity Sheet MT-3: *Design a Castle*, instruct your students to draw a floor plan and front-view of their castle. Write about their reasons for the design: why they chose their materials, what living requirements were met, and what defense systems were included.

Extended Activities:

One of the most famous legends in Medieval Europe was the story of King Arthur, Camelot and the Round Table. Several sites have appeared on the WWW to provide a "sounding board" for sharing ideas on this popular subject. To learn more information on this topic, have students use their favorite search engine or subject directory. Then discuss in small groups the answers to these questions:

1. Is there any historical basis for believing that King Arthur and his Court ever really existed? If so, where were they located?

2. What do you think the purpose of myths and legends were for the "everyday" people?

3. What role did Christianity and the Church play in the growth of chivalry?

After small groups have brainstormed this topic, have them compile a list of appropriate questions for their classmates to discuss and answer.

Activity Sheet MT-3:

DESIGN A CASTLE

Name _____

Plan and sketch a floor plan for a Medieval castle. Draw a front view. Then write a description of what you have designed and why, answering these questions:

1. Why did you choose this particular design for your castle?_____

   _____

   _____

   _____

2. Tell what materials you would build with and why you chose them. _____

   _____

   _____

3. Describe what living conditions your plan allows. _____

   _____

   _____

   _____

4. What type of defense systems did you include in your floor plans? _____

   _____

   _____

   _____

5. What might you design for the grounds around your castle to meet royal family needs?

   _____

   _____

   _____

   _____

THE WORLD OF THE VIKINGS

The Vikings were among the fiercest sea rovers and land warriors who ever lived. Also called Northmen, Norsemen, and Danes, they were a Nordic people, ancestors of the Swedes, Norwegians, and Danes of today. They explored and established settlements in Iceland, Greenland, and America, the latter proving to be an unsuccessful venture. Between the 700s and 1100s, they spread fear throughout the British Isles, much of Europe, and Scandinavia. Sagas have been written about the adventures and deeds of these war-loving, sea-faring people.

Known as the most-skilled of the high-powered shipmakers and navigators, their raiding parties grew from simple plundering and acts of piracy to savage mass killings and burning of whole villages, including the men, women, and children. It is possible that these fierce invasions of other lands may have been to escape the serious conditions at home—political conditions, population growth, and the need for more land and income. It was partly due to a way of life that centered on planting crops in the spring before setting out on raids, returning mid-summer for the harvest, leaving again for more raiding, and returning in the winter to prepare for the next year's raids. The long, cold days were spent perfecting their warrior skills and playing dice and chess-like games.

All cultures and civilizations eventually find a way of communicating information via some form of written language. The Vikings developed a system using futharks, which include letters (runes) similar to our alphabet. The Viking runes served a number of purposes. First of all, they were an alphabet used for communication. Many examples of futharks can be found in Scandinavia and what is now northern Germany. In addition, they could be used in magic spells or in divination rites.

The Vikings were people of great courage and imagination. They were farmers raising cattle, sheep, and pigs. Some were fishermen of cod, herring, and seal. Others were workers in fisheries. Skilled metal-workers made weapons, tools, helmets, and breastplates. In battle, they became masters at quickly building fortifications in the places they had captured. Skilled shipbuilders constructed small, shallow ships about 16 by 70 feet, propelled by 30 or 40 oarsmen. However, some ships are believed to have measured 300 feet, capable of going anywhere in the world. Without the benefit of a compass, a sextant, or other navigational instruments of that time, the Vikings fearlessly sailed their ships across vast unknown expanses of ocean.

The Vikings became more civilized as they learned and adapted to the ways of the people they captured. One sign of their intelligence was their later ability to give up the cruel destructive ways of their ancestors for more peaceful, productive pursuits, switching from being pirates to becoming successful commercial traders.

LESSON 20

INTRODUCTION TO THE VIKINGS

Introduce your students to the Vikings and the area of their European domination during the Middle Ages.

Materials: Activity Sheet V-1: *Viking Travel Routes* (answer key below)
               Copies of the Viking map

Web Sites: http://www.nls.no/viking/e/maps/emaps.htm
               http://www.pastforward.co.uk/vikings/index.html
               http://www.heureka.fi/en/x/nxmyllykoski.html

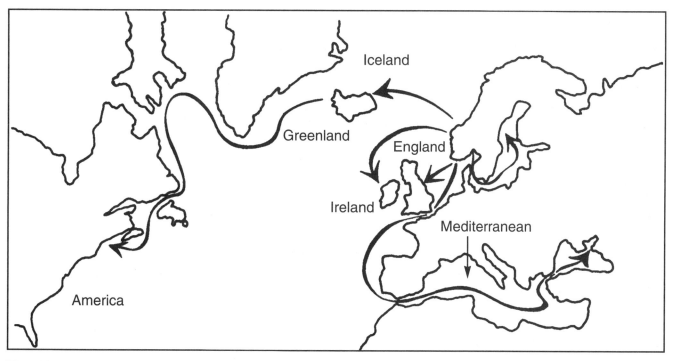

Teaching the Lesson:

1. Have students log on to the Website: http://www.hist.unt.edu/09w-eu0b.htm which traces the Viking's journey throughout Europe.

2. Using Activity Sheet V-1: *Viking Travel Routes*, chart the pathway the Vikings took on their travels and mark which countries they conquered as part of their raids.

Activity Sheet V-1:

VIKING TRAVEL ROUTES

Name _____

http://www.hist.unt.edu/09w-eu0b.htm

1. Using the above Web site and the map below, chart the pathway the Vikings took on their travels and indicate which countries they conquered as part of their "wars."

2. Label the continents, bodies of water, and specific countries involved.

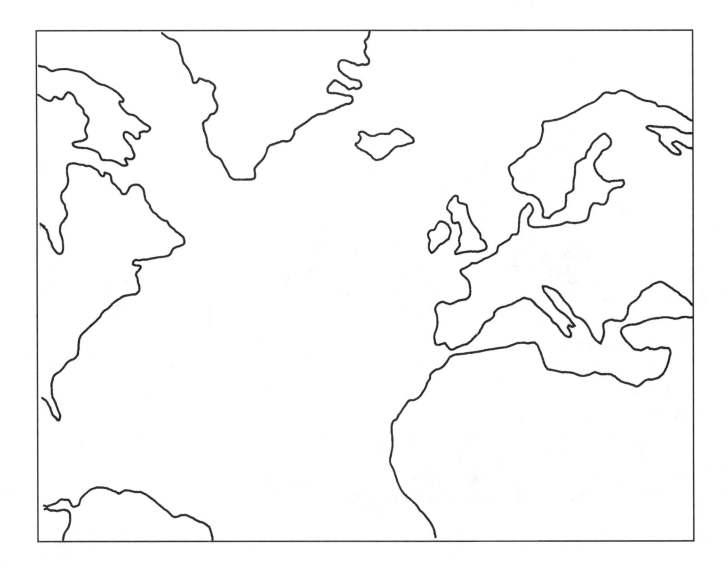

LESSON 21

EVERYDAY LIFE IN VIKING TIMES

Allow your students to explore the everyday life of the Vikings, their social structure, food-gathering, housing, clothing, and family customs.

Materials: Activity Sheet V-2: *Viking Everyday Life*
Activity Sheet V-3: *Create Your Own Viking Jewelry*

Web Sites: http://www.pastforward.co.uk/vikings/index.html
http://www.nls.no/viking/e/life.eindex.htm
http://www.rhi.hi.is/~edg/
http://www.n-vision.com/spoon/vikes/vikorn.html

Teaching the Lesson:

1. Have students log on to the above sites to gather general information on the Vikings' everyday life. Follow up with Activity Sheet V-2: *Viking Everyday Life.*

2. Working in small groups, have your students search the Web sites for a specific category of everyday Viking life that they find of interest.

3. Have them collect all the facts they can find on their topic and decide together what information is to be shared with the class. They need to decide the most appropriate way of visually reporting their information back to the class.

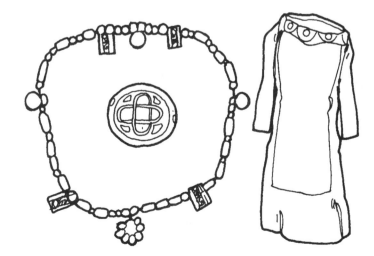

Activity Sheet V-2:

VIKING EVERYDAY LIFE

Name _____

1. Create your own description of a typical day in the life of a Viking at home between battles. _____

   _____

   _____

   _____

   _____

   _____

2. Create your own description of a typical day in the life of a Viking seaman when he was on board his ship, exploring the world. _____

   _____

   _____

   _____

   _____

   _____

3. Create your own description of a typical day in the life of a Viking warrior training for future raids. _____

   _____

   _____

   _____

   _____

      98

Lesson 22

VIKING ORNAMENTATION

Allow your students to look more closely at the areas of decorative and functional jewelry in Viking life.

Materials: Activity Sheet V-3: *Create Your Own Viking Jewelry* (3 pages)

Websites: http://www.eskimo.com/~revoke/ (examples of Viking jewelry)

Jewelry was used to adorn everyday clothing for decorative as well as functional purposes (such as keeping a cloak closed during the cold weather). Brooches, cloak clasps, and hair combs were all pieces of jewelry that were commonly found among Viking artifacts. Most of their jewelry was made of some kind of soft metal, which could be softened by heating or changed by pounding (much the same way a blacksmith makes shoes for horses).

Teaching the Lesson:

1. Have students log on to the above Web sites to examine the types of Viking jewelry, how the jewelry was used and worn, and what the various symbols represent.

    For examples of Viking jewelry, have students log on to the first Web site listed above.

    For examples of Viking burial ornamentation, have students log on to the second Web site listed above.

2. Have students discuss the ways the Vikings used jewelry to adorn everyday clothing for decorative as well as functional purposes, such as keeping a cloak closed during the cold weather.

3. Have students use the three pages of Activity Sheet V-3: *Create Your Own Viking Jewelry* which provides directions for students to create their own jewelry designs and templates using their choice of colors.

4. Have students share their creations with the class. Ask them to share their reasons for the symbols they chose.

Extended Activities:

1. Have students research the clothing worn by the Vikings. Have students create a panel of three drawings to illustrate the seasonal changes in clothing and how their clothing reflected what they were doing. Have students recall the seasonal descriptions they wrote on Activity Sheet V-1: *Viking Everyday Life.*

Activity Sheet V- 3:

CREATE YOUR OWN VIKING JEWELRY

Name: _____

Geometric patterns often formed the basis for jewelry. For women, brooches were considered an essential part of their everyday adornment.

1. Log on to the Web sites below to study some examples of Viking jewelry:

    http://www.eskimo.com/~revoke/ (examples of Viking jewelry)

    http://www.best.com/~gazissax/silence/postmortem/3stone/pmp30051.htm
    (burial ornamentation)

2. Design your own Viking brooch below by using the basic shape and adding the symbols of your choice. Or, you can add color to one of the prepared templates that follow.

3. Cut out and laminate your creation to strengthen your brooch.

4. You may want to shrink the templates before coloring them.

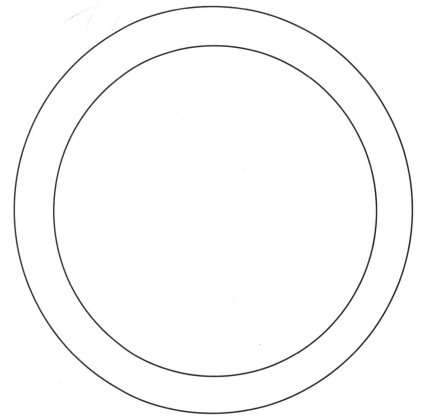

Activity Sheet V-3:

CREATE YOUR OWN VIKING JEWELRY *(cont.)*

Name: _____

With the template below, you can use vibrant colors to create your own Viking jewelry. If you intend to produce an actual brooch, first reduce the size.

Activity Sheet V-3:

CREATE YOUR OWN VIKING JEWELRY *(cont.)*

Name: _____

Brooches, cloak clasps, and hair combs were all pieces of jewelry that were commonly found among the Viking artifacts. With the template below, use colors to create your own Viking jewelry by designing your own symbols. If you intend to produce an actual brooch, first reduce the size.

102

LESSON 23

VIKING RUNES AND FUTHARKS

Allow your students to identify and explore the meaning of the ancient runes of the Vikings.

Materials: Activity Sheet V-2: *Write Your Name in Runes and Futharks*

Web Sites: http://www.algonet.se/~tanprod/wwwinfo.htm

http://www.ugcs.caltech.edu/cherryne/runes.html

http://www.baylor.edu/~Gregory_Randall/rune.html

Preparation: Students should have some knowledge of Viking everyday life and culture.

Teaching the Lesson:

1. Introduce futharks, the ancient Viking system of written communication. Similar to our alphabet, it used a series of symbols, or letters, called *runes.*

2. Have students log on to the above website. Have students study and discuss the information found and compare it to other alphabets already studied.

3. Use Activity Sheet V-3: *Write Your Name in Runes and Futharks* to allow students to try out the futharks alphabet by writing their name in runes.

Extended Activities:

1. Have students search the WWW using an engine of their choice to find other systems of written communication that were used in the Ancient World. Have them choose an appropriate system, write another person's name and share it with the class, along with the key. Have the class try to guess the name.

2. Have students invent their own basic system of the alphabet, creating a simple symbol for each letter. Have them write a brief two word message; then have each student exchange their message with a partner and decipher each other's words.

Activity Sheet V-4:

WRITE YOUR NAME IN RUNES AND FUTHARKS

Name _____

Directions for the Activity

1. Begin by writing your first name in large block letters of our alphabet on the lines below.

___ ___ ___ ___ ___ ___ ___ ___ ___ ___ ___ ___ ___ ___ ___ ___

2. Using the chart below, find the characters that most closely match the letters in your name and write them on the line below. You may need to write phonetically.

_____

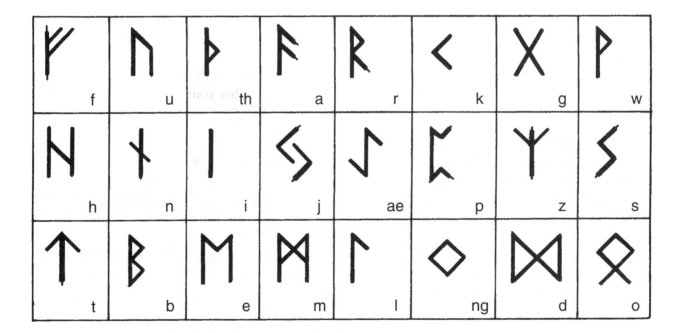

3. Now use the chart to write at least three other words or phrases. When it is completed, give this sheet to a classmate to decipher your words.

LESSON 24

DID THE VIKINGS EXPLORE NORTH AMERICA?
(Greenland, Newfoundland)

Have your students investigate the possibility that North America was visited by the Vikings prior to Columbus's official discovery of America.

Materials: Activity Sheet V-5: *Were the Vikings in North America?*
Printed copy of a map of ancient Vinland from the web site:
http://odin.nls.no/vikings/maps/e/ehome.html

Web Sites: http://www.control.chalmers.se/vikings/viking.american.html
http://odin.nls.no/viking/e/america/evinland.htm
http://www2.pbs.org/wgbh/pages/nova/teachersguide/vikings/

(This site is from "NOVA," a television program, and includes a teacher's guide to the Vikings in North America).

Preparation: Students should have some familiarity with the time-frames and events surrounding the discovery of America by Christopher Columbus.

Teaching the Lesson:

1. Begin by asking students if they know the story of Christopher Columbus and the discovery of America. Follow up with a discussion so you can determine what your students might already know about this topic. (You may need to read them a brief book about Columbus.)

2. After you have determined your students' knowledge level, ask them if there might have been other visitors to North America prior to Columbus. Allow them to speculate awhile before searching the Internet for information.

3. Search the Web sites above to get the opinions of experts on the Viking explorations. (NOVA information includes some reference to evidence supporting the theory that the Vikings discovered North America.)

4. Allow time for small group discussions so students can share their ideas on the questions listed on Activity Sheet V-5.

5. Have the students use Activity Sheet V-5: *Were the Vikings in North America?* to write their final conclusions on the subject.

Extended Activities:

Some sources on the World Wide Web present theories and some evidence concerning the Vikings' presence in North America. Have students use these keywords to find more information. They can add their own relevant keywords to the list.

Vinland	Leif Ericson	Eirikur the Red (Iceland)
The Heavener Runestone	L'Anse aux Meadows	Kensington Runestone

Activity Sheet V-5:

WERE THE VIKINGS IN NORTH AMERICA?

Name _____

Assume that the Vikings were visitors to North America before Christopher Columbus arrived. Might there have been other ancient visitors as well?

1. How might the Vikings have traveled to America?_____

   _____

   _____

2. Who might the other visitors have been? _____

   _____

   _____

3. Do you believe that there were, or were not other visitors? Why?_____

   _____

   _____

4. What evidence supports your theory? _____

   _____

   _____

5. What kind of ships might be used to make a journey of such a long distance?

   _____

   _____

6. Were such ships available at the time the Vikings might have visited North America?

   _____

   _____

MESOAMERICA

Aproximately the same time the European and Chinese cultures were expanding, the native populations of the Americas were also developing their own civilizations. The misnamed American Indians originated in Asia. About 20,000 years ago groups began following the animals they hunted, wandering in several waves across the 50-mile-long, ice-covered land connection that is the Bering Strait linking Siberia with Alaska. By around 10,000 B.C. groups of these "Ancient Ones" had penetrated all the way to the southern tip of South America.

About 2500 B.C., the first great culture of Mesoamerica, the mysterious Olmec tribes, began building large settlements and elaborate trade routes along the Gulf Coast of Mexico. Archaeologists have found religious icons and artifacts revealing ceremonial games and rituals involving human sacrifice that later civilizations would adapt as their own. By 1500 B.C., sophisticated evidence shows that three important cultures were thriving in the ancient Americas:

1. *Mesoamerica,* which includes the modern countries of Mexico, Guatemala, Belize, and upper central America, El Salvador, and Honduras.

2. *Lower Central America,* including Costa Rica and Panama.

3. *The Central Andes* of Peru, Ecuador, Chile, and Bolivia.

It is interesting to note that Mesoamerica and the Andes were two of the six "cradles of civilization," along with China, India, Egypt, and Mesopotamia. Maize (corn) was first domesticated in this area. The development of an amazingly accurate Mayan calendar system and beautifully stylized hieroglyphics can be traced back to the Olmec heritage. Artists created composite beings with human, animal, and supernatural attributes. Working with a variety of native stones, fired clay and metal alloys and using crude but effective tools, craftsmen were able to create remarkable works of art. This included small functional sculptures, vessels, and instruments for massive ceremonial monoliths.

Best-known of the Mesoamerica civilizations were the Maya and the Aztec civilizations who reached their height between 2500 B.C. and 1500 A.D. The Maya worshipped the gods of rain, sun, soil, and corn in vast ceremonial centers composed of pyramids, courts for playing a ball and hoop game, terraces and temples in which only the priests were allowed to live. Known for their artistic and intellectual achievements, the Maya built observatories to study the stars and decorated their temple walls with ornate stone carvings, majestic pillars, and brightly-colored scenes.

Dominating the highland valleys of central Mexico, the mighty Aztecs built large cities. Their capital, Tenochtitlan, stood on an island in Lake Texcoco, the site of present-day Mexico City. It had a community of 100,000 when the Spaniards arrived. Human sacrifice was done on a large scale in the huge ceremonial center, which stood in the middle of the city. Two temples to their gods topped a great pyramid-like structure. Much of their food was grown on mud-covered rafts (chinampas) floating in the lake. Modern Hispanics continue to create a variety of rich art in the proud heritage of their ancient ancestors of this region.

LESSON 25

INTRODUCTION TO MESOAMERICA

Introduce your students to the rich heritage of the Native populations of North, Central, and South America and their contributions in the areas of mathematics, astronomy, and calendar development.

Materials: Activity Sheet MA-1: *Comparing the Three Civilizations*
Activity Sheet MA-2: *The Nazca Line Drawings*

Web Site: http://www.realtime.net/maya/index.html
http://www.adventurequest.com/adven/htm/pics/16600.HTM

Teaching the Lesson:

1. There are two prominent Native American civilizations in the Central American region known historically as Mesoamerica—the Mayans and the Aztecs. In the Central Andes region, another culture, the Incas, developed an empire that stretched 2500 miles from North to South through Ecuador, Peru, and Chile. Well-organized armies and a good communications system supported a strong social and political system.

2. Have students log on to the above Web sites and gather information on the Mayans and the Aztecs. They may use their keyword skills to find more information on the Incas and the mysterious Nazca Line Drawings.

3. Use Activity Sheet MA-1: *Comparing the Three Civilizations* to record your information on a chart. In small groups, allow students to discuss their findings on each culture.

4. Have students use Activity Sheet MA-2: *The Nazca Line Drawings* to try to solve the mystery of the lines.

Extended Activities:

1. Have students investigate topics to look for other locations in the world where mysterious drawings have been found. Following the links at the first Web Site, students can create an "accordian panel" of drawings on tagboard to show and describe these sites.

Activity Sheet MA-1:

COMPARING THE THREE CIVILIZATIONS

Name _____

Use the following Web site to complete the chart below, comparing the Maya, the Aztec, and the Inca civilizations.

http://www.adventurequest.com/adven/htm/pics/16600.HTM

	MAYA	AZTEC	INCA
Architecture			
Farming			
Mathematics			
Astronomy			
The Arts			
Writing			
Religion			
Government			
Language			
Trade			

Activity Sheet MA-2:

THE NAZCA LINE DRAWINGS

Name _____

Like the unexplained origins and stories of Atlantis and Stonehenge, Mesoamerica also had some mysterious lines and geometric figures which cannot be easily explained. One of these mysteries is the Nazca Lines site which is found in Peru. Not much is known about the Nazca lines or who is responsible for drawing them. The markings are called *geoglyphs* and are similar to those used in Egyptian hieroglyphics. Some speculations about their astronomical or anthropological basis have been made. The figures, which appear to be of various animals and birds, are carved into the side of a mountain and can only be viewed from above. Use the Web site below, along with a search using other appropriate keywords, to find information needed to answer the questions below:

http://www.adventurequest.com/adven/htm/pics/16600.HTM

1. What reasons can you think of to explain why these drawings are only visible from the air?

   _____

   _____

2. What is extraordinary about the 619 meter altitude of the location?

   _____

   _____

3. Where exactly are the Nazca Lines located?

   _____

   _____

4. Describe the shapes that are cut into the stony desert.

   _____

   _____

5. How do some historians and archaeologists explain the origins of the lines?

   _____

   _____

   _____

LESSON 26

THE MYSTERY OF THE MAYA

Allow your students to explore information on the Mayan civilization and its subsequent disappearance from its Central American location.

Materials: Activity Sheet MA-3: *The Mayan Calendar System*
Activity Sheet MA-4: *Mayan Hieroglyphics*

Web Sites: http://www.civilization.ca/membrs/civiliz/maya/mminteng.html
http://www.halfmoon.org/writinghtml

Preparation: It will be helpful if students have some basic knowledge of the geography and cultures of the region before and after the appearance of the Maya.

Teaching the Lesson:

1. The Maya were another civilization which existed in the area around what is currently Mexico City from 2000 B.C. until approximately 800-900 A.D. The civilization can be divided into several time periods, the best known of which is the Classic Mayan Period which existed from 250-1000 A.D. It is from this time period that we have most of our information and thoughts about the Mayan civilization.

2. The Canadian Museum of Civilization has put together a wonderful exhibit focusing on the "Mystery of the Maya" which can be found at the address shown above. The links here are well worth investigating. Investigate such categories as:

   Mayan culture   maps of ancient city sites
   language   rainforest
   numbers   links to other Mesoamerican cultures

3. Have students use Activity Sheet MA-3: *The Mayan Calendar System* to learn the ancient way of keeping track of time.

4. Have students use Activity Sheet MA-4: *Mayan Hieroglyphics* to better understand how the written language originated in various ancient cultures.

Extended Activities:

1. Have students brainstorm and search the WWW using an engine of their choice to discover other *modern systems* of written communication. Have them write a simple greeting to a friend. Then have them share it with the class, along with the key.

Activity Sheet-MA 3:

THE MAYAN CALENDAR SYSTEM

Besides the calendars based on solar and lunar observations used by other Mesoamericans, the Maya developed a third method of measuring time, called the Long Count. Long Count dates appear as part of many Mayan inscriptions and have been valuable in decoding the glyphs of the Maya. By studying inscriptions, archaeologists have calculated that August 13, 3114 BC is the beginning date of this calendar. Although no one is sure exactly what this date represents, scholars think that it is the date the Maya gave for the beginning of this cycle of creation. Each event in the Maya world is recorded as the number of days that have passed since that initial date. Today, Mayan daykeepers in the mountains of Honduras maintain the ancient count and predict that this cycle of the universe will end on December 23, 2012.

Cycles of the Maya Long Count			**Modern Calendar**		
baktun	20 katuns	144,000 days	century	10 decades	36,525 days
katun	20 tuns	7,200 days	decade	10 years	3,652 days
tun	18 uinals	360 days	year		365 days
uinals	20 kins	20 days	month		28, 29, 30, or 31 days
kins		1 day	day		1 day

Look at the stelae below. Each shows an important date as it would appear in the Long count calendar. Use multiplication and addition to learn how many days each date represents.

October 12, 1492

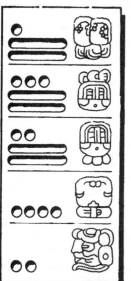

Number of Days

Baktuns x 144,000 = _____

Katuns x 7,200 = _____

Tuns x 360 = _____

Unials x 20 = _____

Kins x 1 = _____

Total number of days _____

July 4, 1776

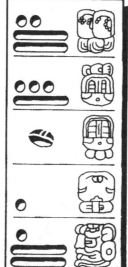

Number of Days

Baktuns x 144,000 = _____

Katuns x 7,200 = _____

Tuns x 360 = _____

Unials x 20 = _____

Kins x 1 = _____

Total number of days _____

Activity Sheet MA-4:

MAYAN HIEROGLYPHICS

Name _____

Deciphering Mayan hieroglyphics is, in some ways, as large a contribution to our understanding of ancient cultures as was the decipherment of the Rosetta Stone hieroglyphics. Perhaps the best source of information on the Mayan hieroglyphics can be found at:

http://www.halfmoon.org/writing.html

1. Log on to this site and make the selection—Culture, Games, Oddities.

2. Explore this site to find a game which you can play with your friends.

3. Make a translation of this game so those who don't understand Mayan hieroglyphics can also play. Draw the game board below.

4. Write out the directions.

5. Play the game.

LESSON 27

INTRODUCTION TO THE AZTEC CULTURE

Allow your students to discover in what ways the Aztecs were another prominent culture in Mexico.

Materials: Activity Sheet Aztec-1: *The Aztec Social Class System*

Web Sites: http://www.cultures.com/mexo/

　　　　　　http://napa.diva.nl/~voorburg/aztec.html

Teaching the Lesson:

1. Even though the social structure of the Aztecs evolved halfway around the world from European influence, they also had a class system with differences that could be identified through observable criteria. A person belonged to a particular social class based upon both his or her personal achievements and parents' class.

2. Instruct students to find out more about the Aztec social classes by searching the Internet and recording their answers on Activity Sheet Aztec-1: *The Aztec Social Class System.*

3. The Aztec gods and goddesses kept order in the world. In return, the Aztec priests gave them human sacrifices to keep them happy. The gods were identified by special clothing and other items.

4. Identify the following gods and goddesses and describe their function in the Aztec Religion and everyday life. Assign students to be ready to share your information with the class in some visual form.

Chalchiuhtlicue　　　　　　Chicomecotal

Quetzalcoatl-Ethcatl　　　　Tezcatlipoca

Extended Activities:

1. In small groups, let students make up the board and rules to re–invent the ancient game of "Patolli" with Activity Sheet MA-6: *Learn to Play Patolli*

2. Have students search the Internet for other ancient children's games which may be of value to children of today.

3. Have students create an "ancient" board game of their own. Teach it to the class and play in small groups.

Activity Sheet MA-5:

THE AZTEC SOCIAL CLASS SYSTEM

Name _____

The Aztecs had a very sophisticated social class. There were essentially three groups of people:

1. *the nobility* who controlled most of the wealth in society including the land; hence they also controlled the commoners who lived on that land,

2. *the commoners* who were responsible for working the land, fishing, and producing the articles for day-to-day living,

3. *an intermediate class* (similar to our middle class) who had less money and power than the nobility, but were not required to do some of the difficult physical tasks required of commoners. They were, in essence, what we now call "white-collar workers."

Use the Web site: **http:napa.diva.nl/-voorburg/aztec.html** to learn about the Aztec class structure. Fill in the chart below. Then, in small groups, discuss answers to the questions on page 116.

Nobility	Aztec Names	Job Descriptions
Rulers: Chiefs		
Nobles		
Intermediate Positions: Merchants		
Luxury Artisans		
Commoner Free Commoners		
Rural tenants		
Slaves		

Activity Sheet MA-5:

THE AZTEC SOCIAL CLASS SYSTEM *(cont.)*

Name _____

In small groups, discuss and write the answers to the following questions:

1. Was there any way to change classes in the Aztec Society? If so, explain how this might be done. _____

   _____

   _____

   _____

2. What advantages would a class-based social system have for maintaining order in that society? _____

   _____

   _____

   _____

3. Are there any economic advantages to a class-based system? _____

   _____

   _____

   _____

4. Would you want to live in this type of social system? Explain why or why not.

   _____

   _____

   _____

Activity Sheet MA-6:

LEARN TO PLAY PATOLLI

(an Aztec board game)

Name _____

Patolli is an ancient board game for which the exact rules have been lost. We do know that players raced their markers around a course which was painted on a mat or on the floor. They used beans as counters and stones for markers. Up to four people played at a time. Each started and finished at "home."

You can play Patolli. Before you start, decide on some rules. For instance, you may want to decide what happens when one player lands on the same space as another. You will also want to know which number you will need to start and finish. A board might look something like this:

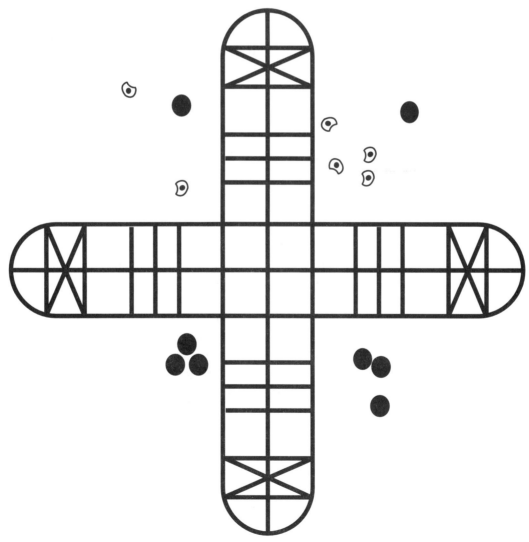

ANCIENT CHINA

Long considered to be one of the four cradles of civilization, it is here that archaeologists unearthed some of the earliest evidence of man living over a million years ago. One of these discoveries, Peking Man, is believed to be an ancestor of many of the peoples of Asia, including the Chinese. Although historians believe it was about 4000 years ago that the first Chinese civilizations arose, the great mountains and deserts kept these early people isolated and prevented contact between them.

The earliest records of China's written history were found in the form of drawings, representing words, scratched on bones. This became the basis for China's present written language. The earliest Chinese writers described an ancient kingdom, the Hsia dynasty, but many believe this may have existed only in legend. Scientists have discovered bones and artifacts from what was called the Shang dynasty that thrived in the valley of the Hwang Ho during the 1500s B.C. As the Shang dynasty reached its power, another dynasty, the Chou, arose, bringing the great Chinese philosopher, Confucious.

Local warring states battled, weakening the Chou empire until the Ch'in dynasty came to power about 220 B.C. Lasting only about 15 years, it brought great change. Shih Huang Ti became China's first dictator, replacing local rule with the nation's first strong central government. Linking the short local walls together, he built the Great Wall of China to keep out other Asian invaders.

By 100 B.C. China had grown in size and power to equal the Roman Empire. Trade flourished between the two giants. Persian rugs decorated the floors of the Chinese emperor's palace while silk caressed the wives of the Roman nobles. Around this time science, education, and the arts thrived. Chinese scholars traveled the known world, bringing Buddhism from India. Chinese writers began producing dictionaries, ancient histories, and collections of classic literature from ancient times.

For about 400 years, China once again was a vast collection of states battling for expansion and control. In 618 A.D., the T'wang dynasty came to power, beginning what many historians consider to be the "Golden Age of Chinese Civilization." The cultural center, the capital city of Chang-an, drew scientists, scholars, poets, artists, and musicians. By 960, Chinese sciences and the fine arts reached new peaks. Important Chinese inventions like gunpowder, the magnetic compass, and moveable type for printing, brought changes that would affect the whole world for centuries to come.

But the Chinese were no match for the Mongol warriors who swept down from the north during the 1200s. Like most of Asia, China became a branch of the Mongol Empire under the mighty and fearsome Kublai Khan. Many European merchants, including Marco Polo, made the long journey to the Far East and returned home with amazing stories of a very rich, highly civilized country called *Cathay*, which today is called China. There followed a revolt against the Mongols. For 300 years, the Ming dynasty ruled and once again the arts and literature flourished. In the 1600s, the Manchus overthrew the Ming empire and set up the Ch'ing dynasty which ruled until 1912. For most of this time, the Manchus forced missionaries and merchants of the Western world to flee, and China remained cut-off and hidden from the rest of the world.

LESSON 28
HISTORY OF ANCIENT CHINA

Give your students a brief history of China and its place in relationship to the rest of the Ancient World. Identify the contributions the Chinese culture gave to society.

Materials: With sound cards, your students can listen to Chinese music and learn some Mandarin Chinese words and phrases.

Web Sites: China's Internet:
http://www.end.org/CND-China/CND-China..95-06-19.html#TOC_E

General Information on Chinese culture
http://www.modor.com/pei/china.html
http://www.ceas.rochester.edu:8080/ee/users/yeung/chinese.html

The Art of China
http://pasture.ecn.purdue.edu/~agenhtml/agencimc/china/china.html

A fascinating country with a long and rich cultural history, China's civilization predates the European cultures and civilizations by 5000 years or more. Major discoveries in thinking and inventions that contributed to the Medieval Renaissance were actually brought into Europe from the East by travelers like Marco Polo. Although an in-depth investigation of China and its history is not possible in these concise units of study, a short introduction to China's heritage is included below.

Teaching the Lesson:

1. Have students work in small groups and log on to the above sites to explore the various options. Have them research the ancient history of China, paying particular attention to artistic creations, scientific inventions, discoveries, concepts, and new ideas that contribute to our modern world today.

2. Have the class list these contributions under student-generated categories.

3. In small groups, have students discuss their findings and decide which they consider to have had the greatest impact on the modern world today.

Extended Activities:

1. Since many people do not understand China and its importance to the United States, use this opportunity to expand the students' knowledge and understanding of the Chinese people. Have students check online international newspapers (both news and editorial sections) for the most recent information. Remind students that other countries' perspectives on the world's political scene are often very different from our own.

LESSON 29

EVERYDAY LIFE IN ANCIENT CHINA

Allow your students to search out information on family life in ancient China.

Materials: Activity Sheet C-1: *Ancient Chinese Family Life/Modern Life*
A wok and ingredients to prepare some Chinese foods (or out-of-class preparation)

Web Sites: China's Internet:
http://www.end.org/CND-China/CND-China..95-06-19.html#TOC_E

General Information on Chinese culture
http://www.modor.com/pei/china.html
http://www.ceas.rochester.edu:8080/ee/users/yeung/chinese.html

The Art of China (includes food, music, art, poetry, and more)
http:/pasture.ecn.purdue.edu/~agenhtml/agencimc/china/china.html

Teaching the Lesson:

1. Have students log on to any of the first three sites and explore the various options, with special attention to Ancient Chinese Family Life

2. Within these sites, direct them to choose a topic of interest to research.

3. Have them prepare a brief visual report of their topic to present to the class.

4. Discuss how family life in China has changed from ancient times to modern times.

5. Discuss how the lives of the Chinese, past and present, are similar and different to the lives of the students. Have students use Activity Sheet C-1: *Ancient Chinese Family Life/Modern Life* to compare the two cultures. Using Activity Sheet C-2: *Ancient China's Contribution to the Modern World,* have students brainstorm words and find information required to complete the seven categories of the chart.

Extended Activities:

1. Have students taste cuisine from another country. A class trip to a local Asian restaurant for a tasting party would allow your students to sample the foods and tastes of China or other Southeast Asian countries.

2. At the *Art of China* Internet Site above, there is a section on "The Taste of China." If you have the desire and cooking facilities, your students would find it interesting to cook some of the Chinese dishes.

3. While sampling the cuisine, encourage students to discuss what they taste, what they like and dislike, why the Chinese foods taste different from other foods, and why the methods of cooking are different.

4. Encourage students to try other Southeast Asian restaurants with their families. Then, in class, locate information and discuss the differences between such Asian forms of cooking as Thai, Vietnamese, Malaysian, Japanese, and Chinese Szechuan or Hunan.

Activity Sheet C-1:

ANCIENT CHINESE
FAMILY LIFE/MODERN LIFE

Name _____

Research and contrast the ancient Chinese way of living with that of our modern times. Jot down notes on each topic in the spaces below. Be ready to discuss the differences in class.

	Ancient Chinese Family Life	Modern Family Life
Shelter		
Clothing		
Transportation		
Kinds of work done		
Fun and entertainment		
Women and Children		

Activity Sheet C-2:

ANCIENT CHINA'S CONTRIBUTIONS TO THE MODERN WORLD

	CONTRIBUTION
Medicine	
Preventive Healthcare	
Architecture	
Industries	
Foods	
Literature	
Inventions	

LESSON 30

THE CHINESE ZODIAC—EARTH AND ANIMAL SIGNS

Show your students that astrology can be approached from a more scientific viewpoint by providing information on how the Chinese determine a person's horoscope.

Materials: Activity Sheet C-3: *Exploring the Chinese Zodiac*

Web Sites: http://www.wlu.edu/~hhill/zodiac.html

Preparation: Computer must have a sound card to do this activity.

Teaching the Lesson:

1. Most anyone who has gone to a Chinese restaurant has been presented with a mysterious placemat showing the Chinese Zodiac signs. These signs are similar in some ways to astrological signs which are used to generate horoscopes. In the Chinese system, your sign is determined by the year in which you were born instead of the month. There are 12 basic signs, each represented by an animal. There are also lunar signs which further pinpoint your personal characteristics. Obtain several Chinese placemats showing the Zodiac and discuss the information given there.

2. Thanks to the influence of the five elements—wood, fire, earth, metal, and water—there can be sixty possible signs in the Chinese Zodiac. Before you have your students explore the sixty new signs, first let them gain a basic understanding of the universe's greatest cosmic forces—Yin and Yang. Yin means female, passive, subjective, receptive, and society-oriented. Yang means male, active, objective, aggressive, and self-contained. Six animals are Yin and six are Yang.

3. Assign your students to complete Activity Sheet C-3: *Exploring the Chinese Zodiac.*

Extended Activities:

Using the search engine of choice, have students locate some WWW resources for Astrology and Horoscopes. After examining the information, have students determine and chart the similarities and differences between Astrology and the Chinese Zodiac.

Activity Sheet C-3:

EXPLORING THE CHINESE ZODIAC

Name _____

Search the Web site: http://www.wlu.edu/~hhill/zodiac.html

The following activities are designed to help you better understand the differences between the different animal signs of the Chinese Zodiac.

1. Write the year of your birth and identify the animal associated with that year.

   _____

2. Read and briefly write the description for your sign. _____

   _____

3. Does the description sound like you?_____ Tell why or why not. _____

   _____

4. Write the name and the year of birth for two or more other family members._____

   _____

   _____

5. Look up your relatives' animal signs and write the characteristics after each of their names. _____

   _____

6. Draw the appropriate animal sign and identify which other influences—wood, earth, fire, water, metal—are part of each sign. You should also note whether the sign is Yin or Yang.

7. From the above notes, write the appropriate information in paragraph form for each relative.

8. Share the information you learned with your relatives and ask them if their description fits. How are they like the description? How are they different?

Further pinpoint your exact Chinese Horoscope by also taking into account some of the animal and earth signs. The Web site above will help you find out which elemental sign affects your sign.

LESSON 31

LEARN TO SPEAK A FOREIGN LANGUAGE

Show your students how the World Wide Web can be used to help students learn another language.

Materials: This is an online activity, so you must have an Internet connection.

Activity Sheet C-2: *Speak in Mandarin Chinese*

Web Sites: http://redgum/bendigo.latrobe.edu.au/~zhang/speaking.htm

Preparation: If you have a sound card, you can listen to Chinese Music as well as learn some Mandarin Chinese words and phrases.

Teaching the Lesson:

1. This lesson can be done as an out–of-class assignment, or if you choose, it could be done as a large group activity using a large TV monitor. However, it works better if students are allowed to work on their own.

2. Learning to speak a foreign language can be an interesting and rewarding experience. When planning a trip to another country, it may be necessary to learn a few important words before leaving. A wealth of foreign language resources for world travelers is available on the WWW. For students to hear the sounds, you will need to have a Sound Card installed in the computer.

Extended Activities:

1. Another use for this feature allows you and your students to hear and learn how to speak several of the Native American Languages such as Sioux, Chippewa and Cherokee.

Activity Sheet C-4:

SPEAK IN MANDARIN CHINESE

Name _____

Use the web site:http://redgum/bendigo.latrobe.edu.au/~zhang/speaking.html

The words and phrases shown below have sound files online so you can listen and learn to speak the language. Your computer will need a sound card. It would probably be best for you to use headphones so you can concentrate on the sounds. Once you have learned some words and phrases, try practicing them with another person.

Phrases

How are You?	Ni hao
Good Morning.	Zao chen hao
Glad to Meet You.	Jian dao ni hen gao xing
How old are you?	Ni de nian ling you duo da?
Welcome to my Home.	Huan ying dao wo jia kuo ke
See you tomorrow.	Ming tian jian
Good Luck.	Zhu ni hao yun
Tomorrow	ming tian

Counting

one	yi	six	liu
two	er	seven	qi
threes	an	eight	ba
four	si	nine	jiu
five	wu	ten	shi
one hundred	yi bai		

Time

What time is it?	Ji dian le?

Days of the Week (Note: some days have no sound files).

It's Monday today.	Jin tian shi xing qi yi.
Tuesday	xing qi er
Wednesday (no sound)	xing qi san
Thursday	xing qi si
Friday	xing qi wu
Saturday	xing qi liu
Sunday (no sound)	xing qi qi

Appendix A

BROWSER SKILLS

In order to successfully access information on the Internet, you and your students must use some type of browser software program. Certain skills must be mastered when using any browser software. All computer operators should know how to do the following actions:

General Browser Activities

1. open the browser
2. follow a link
3. jump to a known page
4. use the History window
5. reload/refresh a page
6. stop a page from loading

Image Viewing

1. deactivate auto image download
2. view/load a particular image
3. load all images on a page

Frames

1. viewing frames
2. saving frames
3. printing frames
4. changing to another frame

File Handling

1. access an FTP (File Transfer Protocol) site
2. download a file
3. save an image
4. save a Web page
5. save a page without viewing it

Printing, retrieving files

1. copy and paste parts of a page
2. print a page
3. read a saved page offline
4. set up printing options

Bookmarks

1. open bookmarks window
2. use bookmarks to navigate the Web
3. add a bookmark from a Web site
4. add a bookmark by hand from a Web site
5. create a bookmark folder
6. edit a bookmark or folder
7. sort bookmarks
8. save bookmark file
9. import bookmarks

Where to Get Browser Software:

Some software can be downloaded from an FTP site whereas other programs must be purchased from a vendor. If you join a commercial service (either a national one like America Online, or a local service), they usually will provide the software (sometimes there is a cost) and help you get it set up properly. If you do not already have access, it is probably best to have professional help in setting up your lines. This will be a worthwhile investment since it will probably save problems later on.

Appendix B

NETSCAPE BASICS

Vocabulary

Netscape Window	menu bar	toolbar buttons
location/GOTO window	open location	directory buttons
progress bar	kilobyte count	autoload
place holding icon	home page	links
bookmarks	header icon	edit window
URL Address	(loading icon-globe)	mail document window

Before you can get on the WWW, you have to get a Web browser. The most popular browser in use today is Netscape. With a browser, you can locate a Web site by using that site's address or URL, (uniform resource locator), navigate the site through the different pages at the site, mark your favorite sites for future exploration, or you can search by topic or keyword.

When you first start up Netscape, you will probably see a screen similar to the one below (The actual screen may vary depending upon the version you are using).

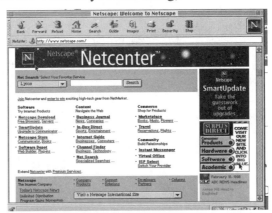

Once you have gotten this screen, you will need to get a particular address or location. Do the following:

1. click on the File choice in the top menu bar
2. select Open Location
3. you will see an Open Location screen:

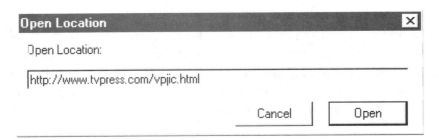

Appendix B

NETSCAPE BASICS *(cont.)*

It will now be necessary to type in a URL (uniform resource locator) or address to go to a World Wide Web Site of your choice.

Search Engines

A popular search engine is the HotBot engine from Wired Corporation. Type the address in the box as shown below:

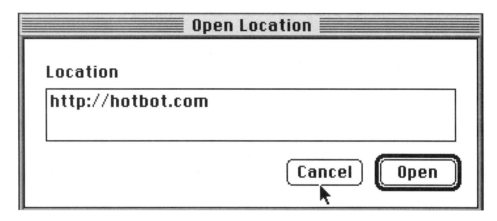

If for some reason you cannot reach the location, a message (dialog) box will appear:

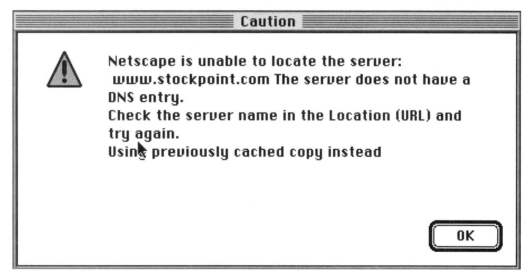

When you receive an error message, there are several things you can do:

1. check your spelling to be sure it is correct

2. be sure that you have included all parts of the address

If you still cannot get into the site, try truncating the address so it shows only the first three parts, as shown above.

Appendix C

MICROSOFT INTERNET EXPLORER BASICS

Microsoft's Internet Explorer comes bundled with many new computers and will eventually be included with new MacIntosh computers as well. The program is very similar to Netscape with the same basic functions and actions. To begin, students should be familiar with the basic vocabulary associated with using a browser program.

Vocabulary	window	tool bar	autoload
	links bar	edit window	header icon
	menu bar	kilobyte count	
	place holding icon	home page	
	URL Address	mail document window	

The tool bar icons in this program are well–chosen and easy to use. The main screen is shown below:

The User Interface	The interface consists of the menu bar and tool bar buttons. A point and click approach makes using the pull–down menus quick and easy.
Menu bar	The menu bar is found at the top of the screen. It has the following pull down menus:

File   Edit   View   Go   Favorites   Help

There are a number of options under each choice. To activate the pull down menu, simply click on the appropriate word. To activate a choice, highlight the choice and then click on it.

Appendix C

MICROSOFT INTERNET EXPLORER BASICS *(cont.)*

Tool bar   Underneath the Menu bar is the tool bar. There is a series of buttons which can be used to move around on the screens. The buttons are listed under tool bar buttons below.

Tool bar buttons   The tool bar has a series of buttons which are designed to perform a variety of functions and/or actions:

Back   **Forward**   **Stop**   **Refresh**   **Home**

Address Bar   This is the location in which you type the address you wish to access. There is also a special Search section in the Internet Explorer which allows you to access several different databases to get specific information.

- Best of the Web
- Today's Links
- Web Gallery
- Product News
- Microsoft

A QUICK TOUR OF THE INTERNET EXPLORER

Locating Specific Web pages:

1. Select **File** from the menu bar in the upper left hand corner of your screen
2. Click on **Open**
3. Type in the address in the address box and click on **OK** (or press the **Enter** key)

Revisiting pages:

1. Click on the **Back** button from the toolbar. Note that this works best if you only have to jump back one or two pages.
2. If you need to go further back, click on the **Go** option from the menu bar to view a listing of the last five sites you have visited. You can then choose the site you want to revisit.
3. If you wish to go even further back, go to the **Open History Folder** choice which is found at the bottom of the **Go** menu. You will be able to find any links you have visited in the past.
4. A shortcut which is sometimes easier to use, but less comprehensive than the History Folder, is to click on the down-arrow button next to the address box. Only the URL addresses are given here so you will need to recognize the address for which you are looking.

Working with Frames:

Frames are "windows-within-windows" which allow the creator of a web page to separate topics and put in separate scroll bars and windows for each one. Each frame can be looked at independently of the others. One drawback of using frames is that you can't save all the information on a page. Each frame must be saved separately.

Printing a Web Page:

Once you have found the information you are seeking, you may want to print a hard copy of the information. Before you start printing, you will have to set the printer options. This will mean setting margins, paper size, and orientation (portrait or landscape) as well as some other options specific to your printer. When you are ready to print, select **File** and the number of copies and specific page numbers (if you do not want the entire document). When you click on **OK** the information will be sent to the printer.

A QUICK TOUR OF THE INTERNET EXPLORER *(cont.)*

A couple of shortcuts which might be useful to you are: (a) to include a header so you can mark the printouts from each search, and (b) to save the URL's you run across in a text file.

To mark pages for printout, do the following:

1. go to the **File** menu
2. choose page setup
3. click on the **Headers/Footers** button
4. Replace the **&w** in the box labeled upper left with **&u**. This will print out the URL in that location.
5. Click on **OK** to accept the changes

One other shortcut allows you to save the URLs that are associated with the underlined text. To do this,

1. Click on the **Print** button
2. Then click on the box next to **Print Shortcuts** in a Table at the End of the Document.
3. Click on **OK**
4. You'll get a printout which includes all the necessary information.

Saving an HTML File

One way to access information if you don't have an Internet connection all the time is to save the settings. You can do this in Netscape by following this procedure:

1. When you find a source you are interested in exploring in greater depth:

    a. click on the **View** choice on the button toolbar,

    b. select **Document Source**

    c. the page will be saved as a text file

Another procedure to accomplish the same task is:

2. From the page you wish to save:

    a. go to the **File** menu

    b. choose **Save As**

    c. select source from the Format menu in the dialog box.

Note that in either procedure you will lose the graphic images when the document is saved.

Appendix D

GLOSSARY OF TERMS

acceptable use	a written policy outlining appropriate use of the computers and Internet networks that is usually within a school district or individual school building
address	the specific location of a particular set of information (see uniform resource locator)
automated search	the most commonly used engines are automated and are used to obtain information from the Web on a regular basis. See robot-driven search engines.
bandwidth	used to indicate the amount of data that can be carried over a transmission line
boolean	a method of combining concepts to gain the result you want using the following "connectors": AND, OR, NOT.
browser	the name given to a piece of software which allows users to access and browse the World Wide Web. Netscape Navigator and Microsoft Internet Explorer are examples of browsers.
bookmark	shortcuts which take you directly to the desired Web page.
byte	a way of measuring data: one byte = 8 characters. Bytes can also be used to indicate how much data is being transferred at a particular speed
cache	a part of the computer's memory that is set aside for storing recently used information. This speeds up the access time when you wish to retrieve the data, since it is stored on your local hard drive.
concept-based	a search for your term plus synonyms of that term (for example if you type in searching "mad cow disease" the search engine will also search for the scientific name,"bovine spongiform encephalopathy")
cyberspace	the name given to electronic computer communications
data compression	data is "squeezed" together to take up less space. This is most often used with graphics files designated-JPEG or GIF or BMP.
dedicated line	a telephone line which is directly connected to the Internet and used only for that purpose.

Appendix D

GLOSSARY OF TERMS *(cont.)*

directory	a "file folder" on your computer which contains files
domain name	the Internet name for a particular computer network or system. These are indicated in an Internet address by the designations: .edu, .org, .gov, .com, etc.
download	a transfer of data (test, graphics, or software) from a remote computer to your computer using a modem or other type of data transmission lines
E-mail	electronic mail-messages which are sent via the Internet
FAQ	frequently asked questions, usually an excellent source for basic information on various topics related to the Internet
field searching	allows searching of different "areas" of the document. For example you could search for the keyword in just the title field of a web document or you might search for headings or an image within a document.
firewall	a combination of computer software and hardware which allows you to deny Internet access to parts of your computer server or networked system
frames	a way of dividing the screen up into separate, smaller windows which can be accessed independently of each other. Frames have their own scroll bars and are actually the same as individual Web pages.
FTP	file transfer protocol—the way in which computers exchange files over the Internet.
gopher	a text-based, menu-oriented system which can still be found at some US Government sites and at a number of overseas sites. They are more common in foreign countries since they can provide faster loading times and store more text materials than Web servers.
header	the top part of an e-mail message which contains information on transmission of the message as well as the sender's and recipient's addresses and the date and time sent.
hierarchical list	See subject directory.
history list	a list of sites which have been accessed through a WWW browser to arrive at the current location. This is a good way of documenting the pathway you took to reach a certain information source.

Appendix D

GLOSSARY OF TERMS *(cont.)*

hits	the common term for the number of matches found when doing an Internet search
home page	the main or index page of a Web site
host	the computer which contains the Internet software and other information pertinent to a particular server
hyperlink	a hypertext link which can be in text or graphic form. Onscreen links are shown with a different color or as underlined text. The cursor will change to a "hand" when over an active link.
Http	Hypertext Transport Protocol-the way that servers and clients communicate with each other on the World Wide Web
hypertext mark-up language (html)	the language that is used to format and create Web documents
keyword	a word, or group of words, that are used to access information in a search engine or subject directory
links	highlighted text on the screen which will take you to another internet location when you click on that part of the screen
log off	disconnect from the remote computer
log on	connect to another computer, usually requires a password for identification
megabyte	an amount of memory space equaling 1,024 kilobytes
menu bar	a sequence of pull–down menus across the top of the browser screen which contain the commands that are accessible for a particular action
meta–index	an index of search engines and subject directories; will do a simultaneous search on many different search engines and subject directories; good for simple searches where a comprehensive search isn't required.
modem	the device used to access a remote computer using a phone line, cable, etc.

Appendix D

GLOSSARY OF TERMS *(cont.)*

offline	not connected to a computer network (local or wide area)
online	connected to a computer network

pathname	the route that is used to get to a particular file. It includes the following components which are usually separated using a forward slash (/)
	    1. the location of the information (Drive letter)
	    2. the directory name
	    3. the subdirectory, if one is present
	    4. the file name with an extension

PPP	Point to Point protocol which allows you to communicate using TCP/IP from your computer and a modem. This is the most commonly used protocol.
protocol	a set of instructions or procedures used by Internet connection software which establishes a standard way of transferring information
proximity	a method of combining keywords to be NEAR, ADJACENT TO, WITHIN X WORDS OF searching the next keyword.
query	request information from a search engine
robot-driven	a robot automatically collects sites on the World Wide Web and the engine creates an index search which is then made part of the search engine database. There is no human intervention.
router	a hardware device for transferring information between networks
search engine	general term for a robot-driven search engine.
SLIP	a Serial Line Internet Protocol; a software program that allows you to connect to the Interent using a serial port and a modem.
subject directories	created by humans (unlike search engines which use a robot to collect information) so the information contained in the directories must be updated by humans periodically. An advantage of subject directories is that since the content is controlled by humans there may be some form of quality control.
telnet	a software program which allows you to connect to a remote computer
TCP/IP	(Transmission Control Protocol/Internet Protocol) defines the Internet. Your browser must have this software for you to connect to the Internet.

Appendix D

GLOSSARY OF TERMS *(cont.)*

thread	a collection of responses/articles dealing with a single posting or e-mail message
toolbar	usually found under the Menu bar; contains various commands and/or actions
truncation	a way of "shortening" a request for file information (see wildcards)
URL	uniform resource locator—the address or location of a document available on the Internet (includes WWW, gopher, and ftp documents)
upload	the opposite of download: you send a file to another server for other users to view.
user interface	what is presented to the user on the screen. Includes functionality of searching (e.g. may or may not allow boolean searching, wildcards, etc.) as well as levels of searching (e.g. may offer a simple search mode screen as well as an expert/advanced search mode screen)
Web browser	see browser
Web page	a page which may contain text, graphics, still and moving images, and sounds linked to other Web pages by hyperlinks
Web server	the remote computer which houses all the web files and software
Web site	a collection of web pages on the WWW which are connected around a central theme or home page.
wildcards	these allow you to search for strings of words or for differences of spelling within words. (e.g. "wom*n" will find woman, women). Remember to use the wildcard symbol as used by the search engine that you are using.
World Wide Web	the part of the Internet containing hypertext documents which are accessed by a browser program. There are approximately four million web sites at this time with new sites being added daily.
window	the screen image
zip	a common term used for compressed files which have the extension zip

Appendix E

BIBLIOGRAPHY OF INTERNET AND WORLD WIDE WEB RESOURCES

Some of the best, most up-to-date, general information on search engines can be found at: http://searchenginewatch.com/

Individual Search Engines and Subject Directories

Alta Vista   URL: http://altavista.digital.com/
Began in 1995; run by Digital; widely-known Alta Vista partnered with Yahoo in 1996; a very large database; sophisticated searching capabilities; can be used for keyword searches and boolean operators (AND, OR); need user to read documentation carefully for the advanced searching instructions.

Excite   URL: http://www.excite.com/
Began in 1995; a large database, excellent section on strategies, lists sites in three ways:

Excite Search uses traditional search engine listings derived from crawling the Web,

Channels By Excite lists sites by topics, approved by editors, has reviews, discussion areas, and

Excite News Tracker lets users search listings found by crawling specialty news sites

HotBot   URL: http://www.hotbot.com/
Began in 1996; run by Wired; uses the same technology that created the Inktomi catalog; rated top search engine by PC Computer Magazine for user friendliness and amount of information accessed.

Infoseek   URL: http://www.infoseek.com/
Began in 1995; well-known; has a separate directory; lists sites by topic, including reviewed and recommended Infoseek Select Sites.

LookSmart   URL: http://www.looksmart.com/
Began in 1996 by Reader's Digest; now on the Netscape Net Search page.

Lycos   URL: http://www.lycos.com/
Began in 1994; the "granddaddy" of search engines and one of the best because of the amount of information it can access; accurate, complete results; a good help section for custom searches; a Top 5% rating service. Site suitable for beginning students: http://a2z.lycos.com/Just_For_Kids/

Open Text   URL: http://opentext.com/
Large database which allows keyword or simple boolean searching; works best when you use the advanced search features.

WebCrawler   URL: http://webcrawler.com/
Began in 1994; site appropriate for beginning students is: http://webcrawler.com/WCGuide/home_and_family/kids/

Yahoo   URL: http://www.yahoo.com/
Began in 1994; the oldest and largest web site directory; check out the beginning student site.

Yahooligans   URL: http://www.yahooligans.com/ which uses simpler interface and categories; has an excellent help section, and "cool" Web site features.

Magellans' Kidzone   URL: http://www.mckinley.com/browse_bd.cgi?KidZone/
Contains a description of the major search engines as well as a comparison of search engine features. For those wishing to get more in-depth information, there is a section on how search engines work.

BIBLIOGRAPHY OF TECHNOLOGY BOOKS

There are literally hundreds of Internet Resource books available at local bookstores and through the regular academic outlets. In general, a few select books will be sufficient for most people since much of the necessary information is available on the Internet itself. The list below contains what we consider to be the most useful Internet resources.

Ause, Wayne, Scott Arpajian, and Kathy Ivens. *How to Use the World Wide Web.* Ziff Davis Press, 1997.

Banks, Michael. "The Internet Unplugged." *Online Magazine,* 1997.

Berinstein, Paula. *Finding Images Online.* Pemberton Press, 1996.

Castro, Elizabeth. *Netscape for Windows.* Peachpit Press, 1996.

Cotton, Eileen Giuffre. *The Online Classroom: Teaching with the Internet.* Eric Clearinghouse on Reading, English and Communication, 1996.

Dimmler, Klaus and Thomas Powell. *Educators' Internet Yellow Pages.* Prentice Hall PTR, 1997.

Eager, William et al. *Net.Search.* QUE Books, 1995.

Educational Research Service. *The Internet Manual for Classroom Use.* Educational Research Service, 1995.

Gardner, Paul. *Internet for Teachers and Parents.* Teacher Created Materials, Inc. 1996.

Goodwin, Mary, Kristin Miller, and Shaun Witten. *Fodor's Nettravel.* Michael Wolff & Company Publishing, 1996.

Gralla, Preston. *How the Internet Works.* Ziff Davis Press, 1996.

Haag, Tim. *Internet for Kids (Intermediate).* Teacher Created Materials Inc., 1996.

Hahn, Harley. *Internet & Web Yellow Pages.* McGraw Hill, 1997.

Hubert, Sherry Gordon and Rich Schwerin. *How to Use Microsoft Internet Explorer.* Ziff Davis Press (A Division of Macmillian), 1997.

BIBLIOGRAPHY OF TECHNOLOGY BOOKS *(cont.)*

James, Peter and Nick Thorpe. *Ancient Inventions.* Ballantine Books, 1994.

Lamb, Linda and Jerry Peek. *Using e-mail Effectively.* O'Reilly & Associates, 1995.

Macauley, David. *Castles.* Sandpiper. 1975.

Macauley, David. *Pyramid.* Sandpiper. 1975.

Maren, Ruth. *Internet and World Wide Web Simplified: (3-D Visual Approach).* IDG Books, 1995.

Microsoft Press. *Microsoft Bookshelf Internet Directory,* 1996-1997 Edition. Microsoft Press, 1996.

Pack, Thomas. *10 Minute Guide to Travel on the Net.* IDG Books, 1996.

Pereira, Linda. *Computers Don't BYTE!: A Beginners Guide to Understanding Computers.* Teacher Created Materials, Inc., 1996.

Pfaffenberger, Bryan. *Web Search Strategies.* MIS Press, 1996.

Pitter, Keiko, et al. *Every Student's Guide to the Internet.* McGraw-Hill, 1995.

Place, Ron, "PC Novice Guide to Netscape: Everything You Need to Conquer the 'Net." *PC Novice Magazine,* 1997.

Roerden, Laura Parker. *Net Lessons: Web-Based Projects For Your Classroom.* Songline Studios, Inc., 1997.

Rowland, Robin and Dave Kinnaman. *Researching on the Internet.* Prima, Online, 1995.

Sharp, Vicki F. *Netscape Navigator 3.0 in one Hour.* International Society for Technology in Education, 1997.

Schwartz, Steven. *Internet Explorer for /Windows 95/NT: Visual Quick Start Guide.* Peachpit Press, 1997.

Shipley, Chris and Matthew Fish. *How the World Wide Web Works.* Ziff Davis Press, 1996.

Tapley, Rebecca. *How to Use Netscape Communicator 4.0: The Complete Visual Solution.* Ziff Davis Press, 1997.

Waltz, Mitzi. *The Internet International Directory.* Ziff Davis Press, 1997.

BIBLIOGRAPHY OF CONTENT AREA

Andrews, Carol. *The Rosetta Stone.* British Museum Press, 1981.

Bateman, Penny. *The Aztecs Activity Book.* British Museum Press, 1994.

Berdan Frances F. *The Aztecs.* Chelsea House Publishers, 1989.

Branwyn, Gareth, Sean Carton, Luke Duncan, Tom Lichty, Donald Rose, Shannon Turlingen, and Jan Weingarten. *Internet Roadside Attractions,* 1995.

Bruce-Mitford, Miranda. *The Illustrated Book of Signs & Symbols.* DK Books, 1996.

Chattington, Jenny. *The Ancient Greeks Activity Book.* British Museum Press, 1986.

Chrisp, Peter. *BBC Fact Finders*: Vikings. BPC, Paulton Books, Limited, 1994.

Coe, Michael D. *The Maya* (Fifth Edition). Thames and Hudson, 1988.

Corbishley, Mike. *The Celts Activity Book.* British Museum Press, 1989.

Cotterell, Arthur, Ed. *The Penguin Encyclopedia of Ancient Civilizations.* Penguin Books, 1980.

Forte, Maurizio and Alberto Siliotti, eds. *Virtual Archaeology: Re-creating Ancient Worlds.* Harry S. Abrams, Inc. Publishers., 1996.

Green, Peter. *Ancient Greece: A Concise History.* Thames and Hudson, 1973.

Hall, Jenny and Christine Jones. *BBC Fact Finders: Roman Britain.* BPC, Paulton Books, Limited, 1994.

Harper, Pam. *Writing Activity Book.* British Museum Press, 1996.

Harris, Judi. *Way of the Ferret: Finding Educational Resources on the Internet,* 2nd Edition, Revised Edition. International Society for Technology in Education, 1995.

Houston, S. D. *Maya Glyphs.* University of California Press, 1989.

Jackson, Ralph, Simon James, and Emma Myers. *The Romans.* British Museum Press, 1986.

Jenkins, Ian. *Greek and Roman Life.* Harvard University Press, 1986.

Manniche, Lise. *Ancient Egyptians Activity Book.* British Museum Press, 1985.

McIntosh, Jane. *Eyewitness Guides: Archaeology.* Dorling Kindersley, 1994.

Miller, Mary and Karl Taube. *An Illustrated Dictionary of The Gods and Symbols of Ancient Mexico and the Maya.* Thames and Hudson, 1993.

BIBLIOGRAPHY OF CONTENT AREA *(cont.)*

Morley, Sylvanus Griswold. *An Introduction to the Study of Maya Hieroglyphs.* Dover Publications, 1975.

Oakes, Lorna. *The Assyrians Activity Book.* British Museum Press, 1994.

Reeve, John and Jenny Chattington. *The Anglo-Saxons Activity Book.* Thames and Hudson, 1984

Sandaker, Bjorn Normann and Petter Eggen. *The Structural Basis of Architecture.* Watson-Guptill Publications, 1992.

Salvadori, Mario. *Why Buildings Stand Up: The Strength of Architecture.* W. W. Norton & Company, 1980.

Sawyer, Ralph and Peter Townsend. *The Ancient World: A Reading and Writing Approach.* National Textbook Company, 1993.

Scarre, Chris. *Smithsonian Timelines of the Ancient World: A Visual Chronology from the Origins of Life to AD 1500.* Dorling Kindersley, 1993.

Scully, Vincent. *Architecture: The Natural and the Man Made.* St. Martin's Press, 1991.

Shaw, Ian. *Timeline of the Ancient World: 3000 BC-AD 500.* British Museum Press, 1994.

Stevenson, Neil. *Annotated Guides: Architecture.* D. K. Publishing, Inc., 1997.

Swaddling, Judith. *The Ancient Olympic Games.* University of Texas Press at Austin, 1980.

Terrien, Samuel. *The Bible Atlas.* Golden Press, 1997.

Watkin, David. *A History of Western Architecture*, 2nd. Edition. Laurence King, 1986.

Whitfield, Peter. *The Image of the World: 20 Centuries of World Maps.* Pomegranate Artbooks, 1994 (reprinted 1997).

Wilson, David M. *The Vikings Activity Book.* British Museum Press, 1986.

Wood, Denis. *The Power of Maps.* The Guildford Press, 1992.

World Book Encyclopedia, 11th ed., s.v. "Ancient Civilizations," "Egypt," Roman Empire," "Greece," "Medieval Times," "Viking," "Aztec," "Maya," "Inca," and "China."

BIBLIOGRAPHY OF COMPUTER SOFTWARE

Although there is not a great deal of good software available specifically for Social Studies of the Ancient World, there is more for Geography and History. In some ways, using the Internet is more cost –effective than using preprogrammed software. With the Internet, the choices are those of the student, not the software developer. Obviously, students need direction, but they do not need to have their choices limited. Computer software is best for developing skills and for providing initial experiences with computers. The programs listed below are part of a series which emphasizes problem–solving and decision–making skills. They are good examples of an open–ended programs which integrate information from several different sources.

Tom Snyder Productions. Decisions, Decisions, 5.0: Ancient Empires

> This program is available on CD-ROM for PC and Windows. There is also a network version available. Topics covered include: Ancient Civilizations, Cultures, Role of Myths, and famous battles. A role playing format is used in which students play the role of a leader if a city-state. As such, they are responsible for maintaining their land areas, pleasing their gods, fighting battles and governing their empire.

Tom Snyder Productions. Decisions, Decisions, 5.0: Feudalism

> This is another program in the Decisions, Decisions series. In this situation, students will learn about the feudal system, medieval society, the crusades and the rise of cities and towns.

Tom Snyder Productions. Decisions, Decisions, 5.0: Building a Nation

> The third installment in this series gives students the opportunity to come into the current century. The emphasis is on the emergence of African Nations.